IT NEVER GOES AWAY

IT NEVER GOES AWAY

Gender Transition at a Mature Age

DR. ANNE L. KOCH

RUTGERS UNIVERSITY PRESS
New Brunswick, Camden, and Newark, New Jersey, and London

Library of Congress Cataloging-in-Publication Data

Names: Koch, Anne L., author.
Title: It never goes away : gender transition at a mature age / Anne L. Koch.
Description: New Brunswick : Rutgers University Press, [2019] | Includes
   index.
Identifiers: LCCN 2018037965 | ISBN 9780813598390 (cloth)
Subjects: LCSH: Koch, Anne L. | Transgender people—United States—
   Biography. | Older transsexuals—United States—Biography. |
   Male-to-female transsexuals. | Transgender people—Identity.
Classification: LCC HQ77.8.K63 A3 2019 | DDC 306.76/80092 [B]—dc23
LC record available at https://lccn.loc.gov/2018037965

A British Cataloging-in-Publication record for this book is available from the
British Library.

⊖ The paper used in this publication meets the requirements of the American
National Standard for Information Sciences—Permanence of Paper for Printed
Library Materials, ANSI Z39.48-1992.

www.rutgersuniversitypress.org

Manufactured in the United States of America

This book is dedicated to those mature individuals
who are contemplating a gender transition. Transitioning
gender will be the most challenging thing you will ever
do, but a successful transition can be accomplished.
The key is to be fully informed and to have a game plan.

CONTENTS

LIST OF ILLUSTRATIONS

FOREWORD

Dr. Anne Koch is announced, and a tall, impeccably styled lady, oozing sophistication with her effortless chignon and tailored suit, takes the stage. This was the first time I encountered Dr. Koch. I thought, this keynote speaker's appearance is reminiscent of a glamorous fashion executive. However, within seconds I realize that we are dealing with so much more than a pretty face!

My "Auntie" Annie is a force—she was put on this planet with enough energy to fuel living several lives, and she has done just that! Dr. Koch's list of accomplishments is nothing short of absurd. Among her many titles are former college athlete, Harvard professor, endodontist, professional angler, inventor, model, entrepreneur, philanthropist, and mentor (especially to me!) and now (finally!) author. Dr. Koch has applied her zest and enthusiasm to every chapter of her life, and her transition is no different. Annie's charisma spills out onto the pages of her story. In her signature, matter-of-fact tone, she frankly describes her transition in a relatable way.

As a cisgender woman and gender-affirmation surgeon, Annie's memoir challenges my beliefs about gender on both a professional and a personal level. With so much wisdom afforded by her incredible range of life experiences, Annie is incredibly authentic. Though always gentle and charming, she is never afraid to voice her beliefs. She doesn't shy away from controversy, and she tells her story with refreshing honesty and insight. While accompanying her on this journey, readers will be captivated by her sheer resilience and unfailing, upbeat attitude.

Having ascended to the top of so many fields as a man, including athletics, entertainment, corporate America, and academia, Dr. Koch now holds her own as a female entrepreneurial powerhouse, and she is passionate about sharing her insights from this remarkable vantage point. An inspiration to ALL women and probably the most frequently quoted person in *my* life, she has finally penned the ultimate must-read memoir.

"She was never bored because she was never boring."

Sidhbh Gallagher, MD
Founder and Director,
Indiana University Gender Affirmation Surgery

PREFACE

If you are transgender, the feeling of wanting to embody the sex you feel you are never goes away. It is always there, like the tide. For some, this feeling is overwhelming. Others try to compartmentalize it and move on with their lives. In some instances, the feeling can't be ignored, and the person transitions. But even when one transitions, it is not the end of the story. Rather, it is only the beginning.

For more than thirty-five years, I was a leading practitioner and educator in my dental medicine specialty. I treated over thirty thousand patients with compassion and concern, presented over one thousand lectures worldwide, founded a Harvard residency program in which I helped train dozens of residents, and created a successful education-technology company. This all came to an end when I changed sex. I underwent gender reassignment surgery at the age of sixty-three! I had no idea how difficult this transition would be.

When I transitioned, I had the unique opportunity to view the process through two separate prisms: that of a patient, and that of an experienced health-care provider. What I witnessed and went through was at times both exhilarating and concerning. Over the past five years, the number of individuals describing themselves as transgender has exploded. As these individuals work their way into the health-care system, chasing their own version of an aligned body and spirit, doctors in many different specialties are being called on to help facilitate these transitions. I found myself wondering whether these patients were being treated properly and with dignity, and whether they were being told the truth about what they could expect. How has the Internet and increased media coverage affected their status as patients? It's a complicated issue, and I decided to tell my story, as well as provide some information I learned along the way, in an attempt to bring some light to the issue, especially as it relates to mature people who might be considering a surgical transition. As a transsexual woman and as an experienced health-care provider, I feel comfortable sharing my observations, but they are only my opinions, and I completely respect the fact that others may disagree. Furthermore, in the interest of maintaining the privacy of people in my life who do not wish to be named, I have, on occasion, employed the use of pseudonyms throughout the book. The use of such pseudonyms will be noted by an asterisk next to their name on their introduction into the story.

I have no political agenda in writing this book. I do not support the far-right agenda, nor do I support the extreme transgender agenda. Proponents of the far-right agenda deny the physiological basis for gender dysphoria and insist on referring to it as a psychological problem. Supporters of the extreme transgender agenda are the polar opposite, viewing anyone who has an opinion other than the total embrace of everyone's right to be in the exact body they choose as being "transphobic." However, I do not bill for services in this area as a physician, and I am not interested in anyone's personal agenda. What I *am* interested in is veracity. The truth.

I believe that transgender medicine has gotten ahead of itself, particularly regarding surgery. Most transgender medical research is consensus based, not evidence based, and this is a challenge, because legitimate medicine depends on actual facts rather than gathered information with implied results. I see problems with trans medicine as it exists today at both ends of the age spectrum—patients over fifty-five years old and those less than eighteen years old. Unfortunately, as the public has gained greater awareness of "trans issues," money has entered the equation. Insurance, including Medicare and Medicaid, is now paying for gender reassignment procedures, and the floodgates have opened. We finally have some surgical fellowships in transgender surgery, yet doctors are still taking weekend courses on phalloplasty and vaginoplasty in order to be "qualified" to perform these procedures. This is not an ideal situation for creating informed and skillful surgeons in this area, and this problem is only going to get worse as more people seek treatment. Buyer beware!

My hope is that transgender medicine will become a legitimate segment of the medical school curriculum. My goal with this book is to offer a cautionary tale to those people over fifty-five years of age who are contemplating a change of gender. Yes, it can be done, but it is difficult to accomplish, and currently there is a preponderance of misinformation and good old-fashioned bullshit out there for anyone trying to find their way. By sharing my story, I hope to encourage mature individuals who are considering a change of gender to re-evaluate their status and to thoroughly investigate other alternatives. There are options available to the mature person other than a complete surgical change of gender. Therapy is critical in these cases and can be enormously helpful.

I am a strong advocate for gender affirmation, and I support the idea of a gender continuum rather than a strictly binary approach. However, I want patients, particularly mature individuals, to be fully informed before they decide to make an irreversible change in their bodies.

IT NEVER GOES AWAY

1 · THE EARLY YEARS

I WAS BORN on December 20, 1949, a Christmas baby. Everyone was hoping for a baby girl, but following a cesarean section, I arrived on the scene. My life as a very young child was unremarkable other than the fact that I loved the beach and loved being in the water. My parents had a summer house on the end of Long Island, which we would visit on weekends and where we spent the summers every year. It was glorious in July and August. So, Little Kenny Koch spent a lot of time in the sun, occasionally getting very sunburned. I was fair skinned and very blond. I can still smell the Noxzema my mother spread all over my sunburned body after I had been in the sun and gotten really roasted. It's remarkable, but it actually seems like yesterday. It's a nice memory.

My earliest recollection of wanting to be a girl was when I was about four or five years old. We were living in an apartment at the time, and my father was a New York City firefighter. My mother's mother, Grandma Annie, visited us all the time, and she was a wonderful seamstress. I had a cousin, Susan, and I remember my mother wanting to make a dress for Susan. At that age, a lot of little boys and girls are the same size, so they had me model my cousin's dress. I stood on a chair so they could adjust the fabric. I remember all the fuss that my mother and my grandmother made about me, and I loved it. I loved the fuss. I loved the feel of the dress. I was very much a rough-and-tumble little boy, but I loved being in that dress, being the center of attention. Sometime later, I asked my mother, as she was doing her nails, if I could try some nail polish. So she put some polish on my nails, which I loved seeing flashing at the end of my fingers. That day my father came home

FIGURE 1. Fred and Little Kenny Koch, East Setauket, NY, 1951
This picture was taken by my mother in front of our summer house. We would spend the entire summer there as well as many fall weekends. I have many fond memories of this particular home through the years.

early from work, and he saw the nail polish. He got so angry! I had never seen him like that. Normally, he was such a nice man. I remember trying to process his anger, but I didn't know what to make of it. I do remember my mother getting frightened and removing the polish. That event "cured" my female feelings, at least temporarily.

The next memorable incident came when I was around six years old. In the mid-1950s, my parents were trying to save for a house. To save money, we lived with my maternal grandmother and grandfather in a place called Whitestone in Queens. Downstairs in the cellar, there were boxes and boxes of dresses made by Grandma Annie, since my mother was one of three sisters. I remember going down into the dusty cellar and playing dress-up and having so much fun. I just loved the feeling of wearing those dresses, and down there, I could hide in the cellar and enjoy myself.

Around the same time, my uncle, who was a merchant marine captain, was dating a German woman who wore fancy underwear. I tried on her underwear a few times and loved the feel of the material on my skin and how pretty it looked. Once, I even got caught wearing the fancy underwear by my relatives when visiting their house, and I was mortified that I'd been caught wearing women's panties. They made a big joke about it, but it was very embarrassing.

I also became infatuated with fur coats. In fact, anytime my mother would go to a department store, I would be transfixed looking at the fur coats. I specifically remember one salesman saying to my mother, "Oh, that little boy is going to make some girl really happy someday by buying her a fur coat." Little did he know that the little boy buying the coat would end up being the girl! I just loved the feel of the coats. I loved the way they looked, and I enjoyed their elegance.

ADOLESCENCE

In 1957, my parents made a huge move. We moved out to Smithtown, Long Island, which was about seventy miles east of Manhattan. Yes, they had finally bought a house. It was such a wonderfully exciting time for my parents as well as for my brother and me. It truly was American dream stuff. The Cape Cod–style house was in a development, and I struck up a friendship with a boy my age. Bobby and I used to play made-up games together. I created a game that included a penalty if you lost. The penalty was that the loser would be changed into a girl. Poof . . . you're a girl! As further punishment, you would have to act like a girl. Bobby and I played this game every day for two years. All of a sudden, poof, poof, you're a girl. The loser would then have to talk and behave like a girl.

At the same time, I was doing incredibly well in athletics, especially baseball. I was also a straight-A student. So, I had this incredible dichotomy in my life at the time, and what is amazing to me now is that a few times during this period, my grandmother asked me if I would like to be a girl. What made this woman think her rough-and-tumble little grandson would want to be a girl? But my Irish grandmother saw something that no one else did. And in those days, in the late 1950s, this "sex-change thing" was getting a lot of publicity. Christine Jorgensen had made a big splash earlier in the 1950s, and there were also newspaper articles about these exotic creatures from France, like Coccinelle, a performer who had changed sex in Casablanca. I remember focusing on any news pertaining to "sex change" for many years.

Junior high school is a confusing, crazy time for anyone. I missed the basketball tryouts in eighth grade because I was taking a piano lesson. I really didn't want to learn the piano, but my mother insisted that I take lessons. Because I missed the basketball tryouts, I didn't make the team, and so I was stuck at home with time on my hands. Consequently, what I started doing was dressing up in women's clothes again. At that point, I didn't connect it to my sexuality; it just felt right. One day, I was home dressing up when my best friend knocked at the front door. He wanted to go to the junior high basketball game. I was wearing women's clothes at the time, so before I answered the door, I ran upstairs and put my boy's clothes on top of the women's clothes. Then we walked to the school to watch the basketball game. There was nothing exotic about it, but I was terrified of someone noticing that I was wearing women's clothes as I sat there watching the game.

By age thirteen, I realized I was a good athlete. In addition to being an incredible baseball player, I was an excellent football player, who could throw a football fifty yards by ninth grade. I got good grades. I was the perfect son. But every night, I found myself saying a prayer, "God, please make me a professional baseball player or a woman." Think about that. As it turned out, I had the option for the former later on, but I was smart enough to not go in that direction; then, the other option came true. It is amazing how sometimes prayers are answered. Truman Capote was correct when he wrote, " More tears are shed over answered prayers than unanswered ones."

HIGH SCHOOL

I loved to dance, but it was kind of awkward in high school because I wanted to dance like the girls, not necessarily *with* a girl. I hid those feelings and suffered tremendous guilt about the way I felt. Thank God I had the intellect and the fortitude to compartmentalize those feelings. But the guilt was always there. It never went away. In high school, all I let myself care about were sports and academics. I had been moved a year ahead in school, so I was only fourteen years old as a sophomore, but I amazingly still made the varsity football team. This was at a big high school—we had more than five hundred kids in my class alone. I made the football team and ended up being the number-two quarterback and a starting cornerback. This was big news! I was the youngest starting varsity football player on Long Island. But at the same time that I was excelling on the football field, upstairs in my house, underneath my bed, I had lots of magazines. Adolescent boys generally have magazines underneath their bed like *Penthouse* or *Playboy*, but my magazines were *Vogue* and *Ladies' Home Journal*. I would sit at my desk in my bedroom and trace the dresses and the women's clothes and then redesign them. I would add a belt or change the color, things like that.

During my sophomore year, I was upstairs in my room, perfectly happy, working on designing women's clothes, when I heard my mother talking to my father downstairs. My mother had been a professional singer with NBC, so she had a voice that projected. She said to my father, "Woody, you have to go upstairs and speak to your son." He said, "Why?" She continued, "He's upstairs, and he's drawing dresses." My father's response was priceless, "So?" My mother got very agitated with that response and said, "You know this is not right. You've got to stop this. Go upstairs and speak to him." And she went on in this way for a while. Eventually, I could hear him start to come up the stairs, so I immediately rearranged the papers on my desk, and I closed the bedroom door so that it was open only a little bit. My father came up and knocked on the door, which he never did before or after. He said, "Excuse me, Son." He never called me that; he always called me Ken. I said, "Yes,

FIGURE 2. Fourteen years old, varsity football, Smithtown Central High School, 1964
The only sophomore playing varsity football for Smithtown Central High School.
I played halfback and quarterback. At fourteen years old, I was the youngest
starting varsity football player on Long Island.

Dad?" He said, "Is everything okay?" I said, "Yeah, everything's fine." He continued, "What are you doing over there?" I said, "Well, I'm actually doing my social studies. I'm doing some homework." He responded, "Okay," then turned around and walked down the stairs. Of course, as soon as he got down to the living room my mother was on him like bees on honey. "Did you speak to him?" "Yes, I spoke to him." "Is everything okay?" "Everything's okay." My dad just walked away. I was so grateful for my dad's response. Indeed, I have often thought about the response of my parents if they had been alive when I transitioned, and I think that my father would have had a much easier time with it than my mother. My father became much more open minded as he aged, and we enjoyed a wonderful relationship.

I was very successful in high school. Besides playing a varsity sport as a fourteen-year-old, I was only the second student in school history to be elected to the Honor Society as a sophomore. I excelled at everything, but I had no interest in girls. I didn't want to date girls; I just wanted to be a girl.

During my sophomore year, I suffered a football injury, which would be the first of many. I tore all the ligaments in my right shoulder, so I missed three games and received a lot of sympathy. But the recovery time also gave me time to think about things. As I went through high school, I ended up lettering in seven out of nine possible sports. I won the school's Most Athletic Award and some local awards on Long Island. But even while I was doing what was expected of me as a young man, I couldn't stop thinking about being a girl.

Eventually peer pressure made me date. My first date was to the junior prom. It was an absolute nightmare, just a horrible date. My father drove my date and me to the junior prom in our Mustang, and I was so mortified, both because my dad was driving us and because my date, Laura*, didn't realize that even though I was dressed like a boy, I was secretly thinking, "That dress would be so fun to wear."

During my senior year, I was being heavily recruited as a scholar-athlete, and I planned on going to Yale. Simple. Yale was very interested, and everything was going as planned when I suffered a horrendous injury. I had been "marked" by another team. They had practiced all week, trying to do everything they could to injure me and get me out of the game when they played our team that Saturday afternoon. I was the quarterback in the game, and at one point I was running down the sidelines and jumped over a player at the goal line. As I went over him, he reached out for my ankle and hit me, and

FIGURE 3. Varsity basketball, Smithtown Central High School, 1966
As a sophomore, I played varsity football and baseball. As a junior and senior,
I played all three sports, lettering in each. My interests in high school were sports
and academics.

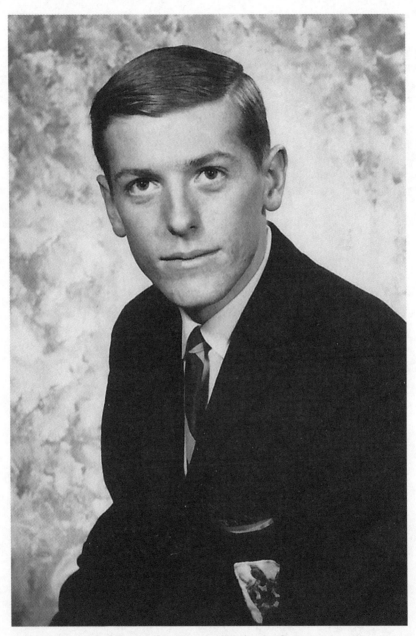

FIGURE 4. Yearbook photo, Smithtown Central High School, 1967
Typical yearbook photo for Smithtown Central High School, Class of 1967.
I thoroughly enjoyed my high school experience and still consider many of my
classmates good friends.

FIGURE 5. Receiving multiple awards from Heisman Trophy winner Major Pete
Dawkins, 1967
West Point seriously recruited me, and in this photo, Major Pete Dawkins is presenting
me with multiple sports awards. I was flattered by West Point's interest in me, but
attending a military academy was not in my plans.

Thursday, April 6, 1995   The Smithtown News   Page 2

Athletes Chosen For Hall Of Fame

By Darren Velez

The second annual class of Smithtown Athletic Hall of Fame inductees has been selected. Delving into the district's long and vivid history, the Smithtown Hall of Fame Selection Committee has chosen to honor sixteen individuals who contributed greatly to the creation of what is now considered one of the finest athletic programs in Suffolk County, a model of consistent excellence in districts across Long Island. As the first class of honorees did, the men and women who will grace the stage when the second class is inducted Saturday, May 13) will represent the personification of the highest ideals of the district and the athletic program, embodying virtues of the mind and spirit as well as the obvious physical talents which they have displayed.

This year's class features a number of individuals who excelled not only on the fields of competition while at Smithtown, but who also led in the classroom and bore the pride of the community with them into institutions of higher learning, where many of the 1995 Hall of Famers went on to achieve great success.

Peter Douglas is one such person. A three-sport athlete while at Smithtown and a bona fide star on the basketball and baseball teams,

Kenneth Koch

which he holds to this day.

Liz Lops

the Smithtown basketball team. His

Dr. William Hayes battled as a member of the Smithtown soccer, basketball and baseball teams, achieving All-League status in soccer and All-American honors on the collegiate level before becoming the youngest person to receive a Ph.D. at Ohio University. The 1967 graduate is currently a well-respected and widely-published poet and professor who taught at Cornell, Cortland and Brockport.

The most recent graduate among the 1995 inductees, Liz Lops was a seminal figure in the development of girls' basketball in the Smithtown area. Described by Smithtown Athletic Director Nick Schroeder as "a big, dominating girl who could also run the floor and shoot," Ms. Lops elevated the girls' game to a new level, establishing a paradigm which later players such as Hauppauge's Maureen Kelly and Smithtown's Danielle Glenn, to name but two, have followed. The three-sport standout was a four-year All-League/All-County athlete in basketball, and a two-year All-Long Island selection. Her 1988 Suffolk County basketball squad and three-year county champion softball team (1988-90) stand as the highlights of the Lops years at Smithtown. After receiving a scholarship to Siena College, Ms. Lops went on to accept an offer to play professional bas

FIGURE 6. Inducted into the Smithtown Athletic Hall of Fame, 1995
In 1995, I was inducted into the second class of the Smithtown Athletic Hall of Fame.
I was conducting a seminar with my endodontic residents at Harvard when a person
from the dean's office presented me with a crystal award and gave me the news.
My residents loved it, and so did I!

I tumbled into the end zone. Then, too late in the play, a huge player came over and kneed me in the back. That got him thrown out of the game, but he had broken five of my ribs, and the ribs punctured one of my lungs, which collapsed. I couldn't get off the field. I couldn't even stand up. Blood was coming out of my mouth, and I ended up going to the emergency room at Good Samaritan Hospital in West Islip. It was a huge news story on Long Island: star quarterback injured; rival player thrown out of the game. It was devastating, with a capital *D*. It destroyed my athletic career and ruined my life. I never really recovered. Since it was such a devastating injury and I was only sixteen years old, Yale wanted me to attend a prep school for a year to recuperate, rather than start college right after graduation. In retrospect, that would have been the smart move. But my parents didn't have the money. Since it was apparent that I wasn't going to be able to attend prep school, that injury basically blew up my Yale plans. When I eventually came out of the hospital, I was shell shocked that something this devastating could have happened to me. I went through the rest of my senior year of high school, but the bloom was gone. Even in baseball, my senior year was the worst year of my high school career. I was still good, but not the same. People couldn't quite understand what had happened to me. But on another note, I finally had a girlfriend, Louise*—Italian American, tall, smart, and attractive.

COLUMBIA/CORNELL/FORDHAM/
ST. LAWRENCE/RUTGERS

As far as my athletic career went, I started to question my future in sports because of my physical vulnerability. Additionally, the feeling that I wanted to be a girl was getting stronger. Nonetheless, everything was set for college. Yale was out of the picture, but I was going to attend Columbia instead. My dad had been pushing for that because he wanted his son to be a quarterback and become a doctor, just like Archie Roberts had done at Columbia. Columbia was interested in me, and I was verbally accepted. But I made the mistake of visiting the campus as a guest of the athletic department for four days. I arrived at 116th Street but had the bad luck to be there when the student demonstrations were starting to kick up in 1967, and after being there for four days, I had no further interest in attending due to all the craziness surrounding the campus. Now I was stuck and had to figure out where to attend school. I had been accepted to Cornell, but my acceptance was in the School of Hotel Management, which I was not very interested in attending. I also had a full baseball scholarship to Fordham, but I was not Catholic— my parents were Protestant—and I didn't know if that would be an issue. St. Lawrence University in upstate New York was a very good school, and it had given me a full athletic scholarship for football. There were other schools in the mix as well, but I wanted to stay in the New York metropolitan area. Finally, after being recruited by one of its agents, I applied to Rutgers, in New Jersey, and got accepted. I decided to go there, and so off I went to Rutgers College, which was an all-male school at the time.

My first year at Rutgers was horrible. Every hope I had for a normal college experience was destroyed. I even suffered acute acne attacks. I said to my parents, "I've got to come home; something is going on." They thought I was exaggerating, but when they saw me at the train station, even my mother, who always had a hard attitude toward me, felt sorry for me. She almost started to cry. I was under so much stress. I was actually putting calamine lotion on my face, it was so broken out. It was horrid.

I had gone to Rutgers to play football, and I thought I was going to be welcomed. After I got there, I realized that they were trying to become big time, like Penn State. They had quarterbacks who were much better than I was. I started out as the fourth-string freshman quarterback, which wasn't bad considering Mr. All New York City was third string, just ahead of me. That person transferred after my first semester and ended up becoming a junior college All-American. I was right behind that guy. The starting quarterback on the freshman team was All-State Pennsylvania. They had really stacked the football team, and I wasn't getting much attention. I was also playing some as a cornerback until I hurt my knee and got a huge hematoma. Subsequently, I ended up spending the second half of my freshman football year in whirlpool baths. I also couldn't stand the locker room.

When my knee finally recovered, the coaches sent me over to the varsity team, as a live tackling dummy. I would go up to what they called "the Heights" at night, and I would return punts. I was the "short man," which is the punt receiver closest to the line of scrimmage. Since I had good hands, they didn't want me to call for a fair catch, which involves no contact, so I was catching the ball and the guys coming down the field would annihilate me, over and over again. Consequently, with all the stress of being away from home for the first time, all the stress of realizing I was not anything special, having roommates, hating the locker room . . . it just destroyed me. Instead of toughing it out, I was crushed. I was just a mess. I wasn't doing as well as I should have been academically, either. So, my first year was hideous.

At the end of the school year, my girlfriend, Louise, went to Colorado for summer school. So she was out at the University of Colorado in Boulder, and I was at my parents' house while they were visiting my cousins in Cape Cod. Occasionally I would speak to Louise on the telephone . . . dressed as a woman, which I still did when I was alone. The fact that some of my mother's clothes actually fit made this much easier. A component of this "feminine feeling" became enhanced when, as a freshman, I went into a porn shop in New Brunswick and found a copy of a magazine called *Female Mimics*. *Female Mimics* showcased female impersonators and some notorious transsexuals. The magazine included pictures of all these gorgeous French female impersonators at the Carousel Club, and I had never seen anything like that. Although I had no opportunity to cross-dress while at school, I found these images sexually arousing. I realized that these were people who thought like me, but at the same time, they seemed beyond the extreme. Here I was, a male scholar-athlete—why did I feel this way? It was so difficult to figure out what was going on.

Overall, my sophomore year of college was much better. I stopped playing football, which helped a lot with my mental health, but I played varsity baseball and some hockey for a while. I was a sophomore in 1969, during the time of massive social upheaval. The Rutgers baseball team also had its own issues. Things were a mess, and we subsequently held a protest to register our dislike of the way we were treated. We staged the protest during a game against our archrival, Princeton. Basically, we just didn't show up for the game. Most of the players on the team were seniors, and the year had been a nightmare anyway. We all assumed that the athletic department would support the student athletes in our protest. Well, it didn't, and the athletic administration essentially told us not to show up for the team anymore. Even though the players were mostly seniors, there were still a few juniors and three sophomores affected, including me. I now found myself in a situation in which I was not going to be able to play baseball at Rutgers. Cornell had been seriously recruiting me in high school, so I decided to transfer to Cornell to be with Louise, who had already transferred there. I was going to study ichthyology. I was going to play sports. My girlfriend was there. This move would solve all my problems. However, the local draft board decided that if I left Rutgers, they would draft me into the army. I couldn't believe my bad luck. I was stuck at Rutgers, and if I missed one semester, they would draft me. That changed my life profoundly. Around the same time, I remember seeing a cover article in *Look* magazine about a transsexual woman getting married. It was February 1970, and I was fascinated. I realized that maybe living as a woman was something that I could do.

By the time I was a senior, I was no longer an athlete at Rutgers, so I decided to take most of my courses at Douglass College. Rutgers was an all-male school at the time. Douglass College was all female, but I could cross-register at Douglass as a Rutgers College student. I loved taking courses there and being "one of the girls." But to make myself seem more masculine, I grew a beard, which my father hated.

One of the courses I took was an economics course with the president of Douglass College at the time, Marjorie Foster. Dr. Foster urged me to go to

FIGURE 7. Rutgers baseball team; Ken Koch, catcher (*front row, far right*); 1969 Rutgers baseball team photo, 1969. We had a very good squad, with only three sophomores on the roster.

Cornell and enter the MBA/JD program. I decided that was exactly what I wanted to do. My father went crazy when I mentioned my plan and didn't even speak to me for a couple of months, because he wanted and expected his son to be a doctor. But I had no interest in medicine at the time.

DODGING THE DRAFT

As I ended my time at Rutgers, I was still dealing with the dichotomy of thinking about being a woman but wanting to be as normal as possible. The first problem I had when anticipating graduation from college was that I had to get a draft physical to see if I was qualified to be conscripted into the armed forces. Before the physical, I read every book I could find on how to beat a draft physical. I stayed up all night the night before; I took my mother's diet pills, which were Benzedrine (speed); and I did isometric exercises. The next day, my friend Richie and I took the bus into Newark, New Jersey, to the federal building for our physicals. The first station was the blood pressure reading. A tech took my blood pressure and asked me, "How long have you had this problem?" I had no idea what he was talking about, but I answered, "My entire life." After we finished that station, Richie said, "What was that? What problem have you had?" I said, "I don't know what problem he was talking about, but whatever it is, I've got it." As it turned out, they had taken an abnormal blood pressure reading: my blood pressure was very high. I had also retrieved my orthodontic retainer, which I hadn't used for years, from my parents' home, because I knew that would give me a temporary deferment. I also had X-rays from my chiropractor of my back. Well, the people doing the orthopedic exam for the army immediately dismissed anything I had from the chiropractor. But between the high blood pressure reading and the orthodontic retainer, by the end of the draft physical I had gotten a three-month deferment.

After those three months, I was called for another draft physical. I prepared for the second one the same way as I had for the first, and my blood pressure was still crazy. They told me that the retainer was no longer active, but I received another deferment because of the blood pressure. A few months later, I graduated from Rutgers, and I was so concerned about getting drafted that I took a few science courses at Suffolk County Community College, as well as at Post College, just so that I would still be in school. I considered applying to dental school for the same reason. However, before the year ended, I got recalled for a third draft physical. They took me directly to the blood pressure station and took my blood pressure. They gave me back all my paperwork and then sent me directly to the end of the room, to a recent medical school graduate, an army doctor wearing khakis. I approached the table; I handed him my papers. He said to me, "Sit down." I sat down. He continued, "Looking at these blood pressure readings, you know you really should be dead." I thought, "Oh, shit, this guy realizes there's something going on. Of course, he's a doctor, right?" He said, "Let me ask you a question. What do you want to do?" I leaned across the table and said, "Really?" He said, "Yeah, really. What do you want to do?" I said, "I'd like to go to dental school." He looked at me, pointed his finger at me, and said, "Go to dental school." He then stamped the application, "Deferred." Done! I was out of the draft.

Many times in my life I have thought how much I would love to run into that army captain who told me, "Go to dental school." I would like to buy him a drink and thank him for what he did. He gave me a pass. He changed my life. I realized in retrospect that he probably got drafted right out of medical school himself. I am certain that he hated being in the army, doing draft physicals. But regardless, he changed my life.

GOING TO DENTAL SCHOOL

Louise and I got married in August 1971, after our senior year of college. She worked as a teacher. I was not working a lot because I was going to school, taking those science classes to avoid the draft, and so I had a lot of free time. I wasn't dressing up as a woman just then, but I would occasionally masturbate, which was something I almost never did otherwise. I wasn't masturbating like boys or men do. I was fantasizing that I was a woman having relationships. But I soon realized, "This is not quite right. There is an issue here, and I better get my act together." I finally decided to just go to dental school, like the army doctor had urged. Maybe that would satisfy my father. When I told him, he seemed to be okay with it, since he considered a dentist to be a doctor. So I applied to the dental schools at Columbia, Penn, Harvard, Case Western, and Temple.

I had my scheduled interview at Penn, my first-choice school, in December 1972. Before that interview, I went over to Temple to meet people there as a trial run and to practice. I went in, and lo and behold, it was the day they were doing some admission interviews. By chance, I got an interview with the dean, Dr. Dale Roeck. As he was looking at my application, he commented, "You have great board scores. Where else are you applying?" I said, "I'm applying to Penn, Columbia, Harvard, and Case Western." He said, "Listen, you are going to get into Penn." I said, "What?" He said, "You are going to get into Penn." He asked, "Where do you want to go to school?" I said, "My first choice?" He said, "Yeah, your first choice; be honest with me." I said, "My first choice is Penn." He again said, "You're going to get into Penn. If you don't get into Penn, call me. We'll take you at Temple." As the dean predicted, I actually got accepted to Penn via early admission, and ultimately, I ended up going there. As it turned out, that was a very good decision.

2 · DENTAL SCHOOL AND THE PROFESSIONAL YEARS

PHILADELPHIA

I enjoyed being at the University of Pennsylvania for dental school. Not only did I enjoy my classes, but I also enjoyed being back on a college campus. My second year in dental school was more difficult than the first, though, because I was married and because I worked three jobs while also attending classes. For one of my jobs, I worked as the clinical pharmacist for the university. During lunchtime, I would change all the cold sterilization solutions in the dental clinics and monitor the ethyl alcohol according to federal requirement. I worked in the dining service as well, and on weekends, I would go back to Montauk (fishing mecca of the Northeast) on Long Island and work as a commercial rod and reel fisherman. I also worked (as a scab, sadly) at the dental school anytime they had a strike and needed custodial work. Additionally, during my third year, I added another weekend job, working in a delicatessen on Baltimore Avenue in West Philadelphia. During that year, Louise, my wife, decided that she also wanted to go to dental school, so she enrolled as well, and we were both going at the same time.

During my senior year, I discovered something in Philadelphia called the Henri David Halloween Ball, which is still being held. At the time, it was at the fabulous Warwick Hotel. The organizers of the ball held a costume contest with awards in such categories as Most Beautiful Female Impersonator, Most Believable Female Impersonator, and Best Celebrity Impersonation.

FIGURE 8. Yearbook photo, University of Pennsylvania School of Dental Medicine, 1977
Classic yearbook photo for the University of Pennsylvania School of Dental
Medicine, Class of 1977. Please note the jacket—the seventies were a brutal decade
for fashion!

Having never seen such an event, I had to attend. I was able to convince my wife to join me, and we ended up going with two other couples. The best thing about the Halloween Ball was the theme, "Don't come as you are, but as you want to be." Like many gay events, instead of starting at midnight it started at one in the morning, and it went all night. At the ball, I had the opportunity to see a lot of very stunning transgender/transsexual people up close for the first time, and it gave me hope for what I might achieve someday. The prize in those years for the Most Believable Female Impersonator was that Henri would pay for that person's "sex-change" operation at Pennsylvania Hospital. This was in 1976, but there was a doctor at that hospital doing the procedure.

I graduated from dental school in 1977. My wife was finishing up her dental degree, and I worked for a Philadelphia health clinic in West Philadelphia. One day, while working in the clinic, I had a young girl as a patient for some cosmetic dentistry. She looked like Diana Ross, but when she checked out, my assistant came up to me and said, "I think the patient has the wrong DPA (Department of Public Assistance) card." That was because it had a male name.

I broached the subject with the patient: "Excuse me, but I think you may have your brother's DPA card." I read her the boy's name.

She said, "Oh, no. That's me." I eventually developed a strong doctor-patient relationship with her, because she needed more dental work, and then very quickly I became the cosmetic dentist for all the black queens in West Philadelphia. They were very happy to have a health-care provider who treated them with respect and who also had a sense of humor. I did not dare mention anything to them of my inner thoughts. One of them introduced me to her mother and invited me to the Henri David Halloween Ball. Even though I had previously attended, I was eager to go again. She won first prize, and I believe she ended up transitioning completely.

THE JAPAN EXPERIENCE

Louise graduated from dental school in 1979, and we decided to go into the armed services. Even though I had fought to beat the draft, my wife thought it would be great dental training and a chance to see the world. Additionally, since my private practice experience wasn't going so well, I thought it was a good idea. We ended up in the air force, assigned to a base in Japan called Yokota, in the Tokyo suburbs. We spent one day on the base and then ended up renting a house in the Japanese community. I loved Japan then, and I still love Japan. It is a feminine country, from the way the women dress, especially the nylons they were wearing at the time, to the way Japanese baseball players are given a bouquet of flowers when they hit a home run. The culture was just stunning to me, and there was so much to learn. Also, at this time, Louise and I were having marital problems because I had no sexual interest in her. This was so sad, because she was a very attractive woman. She was beautiful and smart, but she had a husband who had no interest in her sexually. She wanted to go to marriage counseling, but I refused because I knew what the problem was. The problem was that I wanted to be a woman! Even though I had no same-sex attraction to men, I couldn't help thinking that I wanted to be a woman, and that kept me from wanting to make love to her as a man. But I couldn't say that. So, I just let her think that I wasn't in love with her anymore, and we eventually got a divorce. The split was amicable but difficult. I had known her since seventh grade, and it was hard to let go of that history.

While I was going through the divorce, I also discovered that Japan had a whole transsexual subculture. Transsexuality was far more accepted and in the public view than it was in the States. The Japanese call transsexual individuals the "new half." In retrospect, I think the combination of being in an exotic country, having new experiences, witnessing the intensity of the femininity of my surroundings, and dealing with my secret desire to be a woman accumulated to the point that I had to get a divorce. This was devastating for Louise, and I feel guilty about the dissolution of our marriage to this day.

In addition to my work in the air force, I enjoyed the clubs in downtown Tokyo. One time while I was out, someone said to me, "Have you ever thought about doing any modeling or commercials?" They gave me the name of a modeling agency, and when I went, the agents took some pictures and seemed pleased. Later that week, the agency sent me out on a couple of "look-sees," or what you might call auditions. Low and behold, I scored a couple of commercials and a print job the first three times I went out. The agency was pleasantly surprised, so they took more pictures and created a "card" for me. Suddenly I became a commercial TV actor and a professional model in addition to my work for the air force. Over the next four years, from 1981 to 1985, I did some thirty major commercials, including the Japanese Commercial of the Year in 1983. I was known among the casting directors in Japan

FIGURE 9. Casio television commercial, Tokyo, Japan, 1983
I did many television commercials in Japan, and this was the most famous.
It was a nude commercial for Casio watches. Subsequently, it won many awards,
including Commercial of the Year.

as "the man of a thousand faces." I could do all kinds of different characters,
and I would really get into the parts.

One time, I did a cookie commercial in Okinawa, and I had to stay there
for a few days because we had some weather challenges. There was a stylist
working on the commercial who spoke some English, and she had a friend
with her who happened to be a beauty contest titleholder. I tried to charm
her; I wasn't getting too far, but we exchanged numbers. The cookie commercial wrapped, and I went back up to Tokyo. A few weeks later, I received
a phone call from the girl, Junko.* She spoke some English, and between her
English and my Japanese, the message was clear. She said, "Ken-san, I'm coming up to Tokyo, and I would like to see you."

I said, "Wonderful, that's great. What are you doing in Tokyo?"

She answered, "I'm doing a modeling job, but I'd like to see you."

I said, "That's terrific. Where are you staying?"

And in *perfect English*, she said, "At your place!"

I met her at the airport, and to impress her, I picked her up in my in-
country custom Mazda RX7. It looked like a Maserati. Junko and I drove to

FIGURE 10. On location for commercial, Hokkaido, Japan, 1983
My personal favorite, this television commercial for a coffee creamer had me playing
one of the Wright brothers. It was a gorgeous commercial, as it used a full mock-up
of the Kitty Hawk plane and was filmed on location in Hokkaido, Japan.

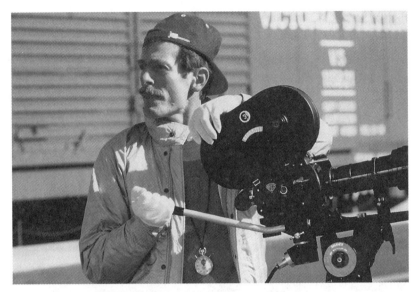

FIGURE 11. Editorial photo, Fuji Film, Tokyo, Japan, 1984
I was known as "the man of a thousand faces" among casting directors in Japan.
This was an editorial shot for Fuji Film in Tokyo. I was not directing; I was acting!

my house, got inside the doorway, and that was it—we just dropped the bags and were all over each other. I had never had an experience like that in my life! Up until that point, any time I had sex with women I had to imagine things, even imagining that I was the woman myself. I just couldn't perform "naturally" as a guy. Now, here I was with this woman, and I had no problem performing as a guy, all night long. It was so incredible and so much fun; I was totally exhausted. However, I was never able to reproduce that feeling again, either with Junko or with anyone else in my life. But I am so thankful for that one night, because it really gave me the experience of knowing what it was like to feel like a guy. It also made me cognizant of how different my normal feelings and experiences were to those of other men.

THE NEW HALF

I dated Junko for a couple of years. I was truly in love with her, but the pressure of her being a beauty title holder and having to bear the stigma of dating a foreigner became too much for us. I even got a call one time from some yakuza who threatened me. It wasn't Junko's fault; it was just that there were a lot of people in Okinawa who had tremendous pride in her.

I also dated a lot of athletes, but one in particular sticks out in my memory. Her name was Tomoko,* and she was a member of the Japanese national ski team. One night we were in her apartment in Tokyo and we were having sex, when all of a sudden, she said to me, "Ken-san, you're gay. It's okay." And she kind of pushed me away. She repeated, "You're gay. It's okay." I was stunned. I thought, "Wow, this is a really experienced young woman if she can figure out that I'm hiding something, even if she didn't quite figure out what it was." I denied it. I tried to explain my way out of it. But she was having none of my explanations. She said again, "No, you're gay. It's okay." Obviously, that terminated *that* relationship.

Regardless of that experience, I continued to lead what I thought was a charmed life in Japan. I was unique in Tokyo. The Japanese were kind to me and were genuinely pleased that I liked their country and culture. Soon, I also discovered what they called "new half" bars. Every Japanese city has a "gay section." The gay section has leather bars along with gay men's and lesbian bars. But they also have what they call "gay bars," which are generally show bars, where they have gorgeous transvestite and transsexual entertainers. Japan has a whole culture of transsexual women, and I found the same in other Buddhist countries, like Thailand. The difference between Japanese transsexual women and those of the West is that the transsexual women in Japan—including the ones who were working, unbeknownst to many, as female models—all wanted to be Audrey Hepburn. They were not politically motivated and made a conscious effort to avoid being seen as coarse. A lot of them had made the change very early in life, at seventeen or eighteen years old. Many of them had gone to Thailand or Singapore for the surgery, and to them, being a woman was about being feminine, charming, and beautiful. The first night that I saw these entertainers, I was at a bar with a girl from my ski club. The entertainers knew of me from my commercials, and when they learned that I was the same person, they made a big fuss. Around two o'clock in the morning, my date and I left, and afterward, she went home. However, I went back to the bar, because I knew they would be open until four. They were surprised to see me return but invited me back into the club. After the club closed for the evening, I went back to my room at the Washington Hotel in Shinjuku, where I would stay if I had been drinking. I closed the door and . . . I started to cry. The discovery of this new culture made me reevaluate

FIGURE 12. My favorite photo of Ken Koch, Long Island, NY, 1986
Taken at a friend's wedding on Long Island in 1986. Not only is this my favorite photo
of my male self; it is how I remember Ken Koch. I still like to wear tuxedos, but now
I add heels and some fancy jewelry!

my place in the world. I realized, "Oh my God, the ability to change sex *does* exist." One of the things I had to bring myself to admit was that even though I was living successfully as a man, I actually, for real, wanted to be a woman. It suddenly seemed like a possibility, where none had existed before. I was finally home. But I wasn't ready to let myself believe yet.

In my attempt to solve my problem, I ended up dating a beautiful transsexual woman, who worked in a show bar. Her name was Ayako,* and she also worked as a legitimate model. The sex was incredible, because it was the closest that I had ever been to being what I wanted to be: a woman making love. I did not have to act or pretend with Ayako; I could share my full emotional range. In fact, six months later, I separated from the air force, and Ayako returned with me to the States. I bought a new car, and she and I drove from Oakland, California, back to New York. Along the way, we stopped in Trinidad, Colorado, which was the home of Dr. Stanley Biber, the leading sex reassignment surgeon at the time. I checked out his office there, but I did not have the nerve to go in. I was also trying to parse my feelings about Ayako, so I had made some stupid excuse about visiting Trinidad. I realized that I didn't truly love her. I had thought that by being with a transsexual woman romantically, it would alleviate my feelings of wanting to change my own gender. Instead, I began to realize that those feelings were far more established than I had thought. Nonetheless, I had foolishly thought that maybe we could solve my issue by being together. On Halloween, we even went down to the Halloween Ball in Philly, and of course, she won all the contest prizes. But the relationship ultimately became a nightmare. We realized that we both had the same personality, and it wasn't going to work. So, after a few months together in the States, I gave her a fair amount of money, and she went out to Los Angeles and, eventually, back to Japan.

A PERIOD OF UPHEAVAL

Things in New York didn't work out well. I was trying to establish a dental business with Japanese companies, but I couldn't make it work. My idea was to offer dental services directly to the Japanese companies in New York, but I needed a Japanese connection on the New York side. Unfortunately, even though I still think it was a good idea, I just couldn't put it together logistically. Consequently, I decided to go back into the service, go back to Asia, and at the end of my second military commitment, I would change gender. This was in 1987, when I was thirty-seven. I made a deal with the air force that would let me go back to Japan after one year in Korea.

When I arrived in Korea, my initial treatment was not so kind by my air force colleagues. They had all heard about my modeling career and wouldn't let me forget it. I had even stopped practicing dentistry when I was trying to do some modeling in New York, so when I showed up in the clinic in Korea, I hadn't cut a tooth in a year. Naturally, for my first patient, the jealous doctors gave me a screaming kid who needed a root canal. I went ahead and did the root canal, 1-2-3, no problem, and they were completely surprised. Afterward, they invited me to a dinner with the Korean doctors working at the hospital. They thought I might somehow feel uncomfortable, but one of the older female physicians knew Japanese, and I spoke with this woman all night long. I eventually became chief of prosthodontics, and I was also the officer in charge of the dental lab for the entire Pacific. I started doing big cases, and I also did a lot of root canals, including on six dogs. Doing veterinary endodontics was fun, and it was made necessary by the decision to eliminate the Air Force Veterinarian Corps.

One of the things I also did while in Korea, as I had promised myself, was make a commitment to change gender. You could buy hormones over the counter there, which I did. I started taking Premarin, an estrogen taken from horses. Finally taking the estrogen gave me great peace of mind because I felt more like I was now on the road to a possible gender change. I bought women's clothes. I also bought a wig of real human hair. I would dress up in my apartment, and as I was not very muscular at the time, I soon realized that I might actually be able to pull this off. I never wore my female outfits in public because I was terrified of being discovered and losing my job. I was simply getting comfortable with seeing my female self privately. After my year was up, I left Korea and went back to Japan.

This time in Japan, my experience was very different from my first stay. It was very modest, because it was just a temporary period until I went back to the States, and then, I thought, I would think seriously about my gender change. However, once I was back in Japan, I began to reconsider my gender plans again. Perhaps there was a way that I could straddle both genders and not be forced to change sex. I figured that I would have sufficient time to evaluate the different options, but I ended up meeting a dental hygienist who worked in the hospital, Akiko,* and fell in love. I can still remember her pick-

FIGURE 13. Air force formal event, Osan, Korea, 1987
Following my re-enlistment in the air force. Note the change in my appearance.
I shaved off my trademark moustache, as I had made the commitment in my mind
to eventually change gender.

FIGURE 14. Air force medical officer, Osan, Korea, 1987
Typical air force medical officer in front of the hospital at Osan, Korea. I was chief of
prosthodontics, and I did an enormous number of cases while stationed there.

ing me up for work on rainy mornings because she lived nearby. It's very emotional for me to think of those times. I would often go skiing with her and her friends. I particularly remember that when I left to return to the States, Akiko visited me at the air terminal, and as we said goodbye, one big tear rolled down her cheek. I will never forget that, as it was the only time a person ever shed a tear for me. It's a very emotional thing for me to remember.

BECOMING BOLDER BACK IN THE STATES

I was assigned to McGuire Air Force Base, near Trenton, New Jersey, on my return to the United States. I became chief of prosthodontics there and had a great working situation, as well as a gorgeous townhouse in Marlton, New Jersey. I started buying women's clothes. I was dressing as a woman on weekends, but only in the house. I kept my body shaved, and I was trying to lead my life in as feminine a way as possible. I was getting emboldened by these small successes, and I even went to a makeup counter one time. I told the saleswoman that I was going to be acting in a summer play up in Cape Cod. She didn't buy that story, but she had no trouble showing me the different products they carried.

I didn't have much of a social life, but on occasion I would go to New Hope, Pennsylvania, an artistic-gay area with a couple of drag shows. I would enjoy myself, just by myself—I never brought a date. I used to watch some of the entertainers, realizing that I could probably do what they were doing.

As a dentist at McGuire, I did a lot of fancy cosmetic work. Once, a female dentist, on whom I had done some beautiful work, was having a cup of coffee with me in the break room when she said, "Ken, don't take this the wrong way, but you have hands just like a woman." Trans people, believe me, *never* forget such comments. I was thrilled.

While working at McGuire, I started preparing myself for undergoing a change of gender. I had stopped taking hormones in Japan, but I began taking them again in small doses while at McGuire. I spoke with people in a Pennsylvania support group called Renaissance, and they offered the opinion that I could clearly pass as a woman. Consequently, I came up with two possible paths forward. I decided to either go to medical school and then change gender, or go to an endodontic training program and not transition. My thinking was the following: If I changed gender, it would be difficult getting reestablished in my field, as dentistry is more conservative than medicine. However, I thought going to medical school and concentrating on facial aesthetics (plastic surgery) would give me a new start. On the other hand, even though I was already a dental specialist and doing prosthodontics (full mouth reconstruction), I really wanted to be an endodontist (working on the inside of the tooth). That was what I truly loved doing. But if I stayed in dentistry, I simply could not imagine changing gender and finding a job. Therefore, I decided that fate could show her hand if I applied to only one endodontic program; if I got accepted, that meant I was supposed to stay in dentistry and not change gender. So that's what I did. I applied to the best endodontic program, the most competitive to get into, which just happened to be at the University of Pennsylvania, my dental school alma mater. I was accepted, so I put my gender change aside and decided to go back to Philly. I planned on separating from the air force for a second time, but I got held over due to Desert Storm. Subsequently, I left the air force on the Friday before Labor Day, and I entered endodontic training on the following Tuesday. I have never regretted that decision for one second. I have treated tens of thousands of patients. I've done twenty thousand-plus endodontic procedures. I've created products and techniques that have been used in millions of cases. I am very proud of those accomplishments. Of course, I have thought many times, what would have happened if I had gone in the other direction? I don't know if I could have gotten into the allopathic medical program of my choice, but I am very confident that I could have gotten into an osteopathic medical school. However, I think I made the right decision at the time.

When I left the air force to begin endodontic training, I also started to wear clear nail polish and women's underwear. It was my way of inserting a little bit of femininity into my everyday life without raising any red flags, but people did notice the nail polish. During the first semester of my endodontic residency, I also made the decision to get married to Akiko. After I left Japan, she came to visit me a few times, and it was always wonderful. I even took her out to Long Island to meet my parents. However, as I continued to lead my life in a more feminine manner, I realized that relationships were going to get very complicated. Akiko definitely wanted to get married and join me in New Jersey, where I was living. Since I had made the decision to enter endodontic training rather than change gender, I thought that I would be able to bury my feminine aspirations. Nonetheless, before we got married, I wrote

Akiko a letter. In the letter, which I wrote in English but translated for her into Japanese, I mentioned that since I had been five years old I felt like I wanted to be a woman. I told her that I didn't think the issue would stand in the way of the marriage, and that my feelings might just stay in their place, but I couldn't guarantee that, and I wanted her to know. I thought I was the only person ever to write such a letter, but years later I learned that it was a fairly common thing for transsexual women to do, especially if the transition comes later in life. This is because there is enormous guilt that this desire is such a powerful compulsion, and someone who is supposed to be your life partner really should know what you're feeling. Akiko's response to my letter was fairly bland; in fact, she said that she preferred feminine-type guys. That was a surprise to me, but it seemed encouraging. We got married on the Penn campus on December 20, 1991. To test out our new understanding, on my wedding night I wore a pair of women's pajamas. I wanted to see how Akiko reacted. It was not an issue for her.

MY ENDODONTIC CAREER

After I graduated from Penn in 1993, Akiko and I moved up to Boston, and I became a full-time faculty member at Harvard. I was asked to create a new postdoctoral program in endodontics. I loved the teaching aspect. I averaged almost eighty hours a week at the school. Life was busy, and I appreciated my spouse. I was always at the school, and I was making very little money, but I loved what I was doing. At the same time, Akiko was employed at the Coach store in Quincy Market, working principally with Japanese tourists. She had some other Japanese friends, and we both seemed to be enjoying the Boston experience. I particularly appreciated the fact that after evening sessions in the dental school, she would pick me up.

I continued my association with Harvard for five years before taking a job in 1998 as a director with the world's largest endodontic company, Tulsa Dental, where I was asked to create an education division. We moved out to Tulsa, Oklahoma, for my new job, which was in all ways a culture shock. I did enjoy the job, however. I learned the company from every angle: I went on sales calls with the reps, I went to the original equipment manufacturers, I learned about the patents. The job became my MBA. In fact, one year I gave 175 lectures.

FIGURE 15. Dr. Ken Koch lecturing for Real World Endo, 2011
As the founder and past CEO-president of Real World Endo, I have presented more
than one thousand lectures worldwide in my career. I love teaching and enjoy
lecturing. This period was a happy time in my life.

Eventually, I left my job at Tulsa and started my own company. I created Real World Endo initially as an education company, and I gave endodontic lectures on cruise ships for doctors and at dental conferences. Soon, I brought in a business partner, and we started to develop innovative dental products and techniques. Before we knew it, Real World Endo became very successful, and we were approached by a larger company to create and share an endodontic division with them.

A HUGE WAKE-UP CALL

By 2005, Akiko and I had two beautiful homes. We had a house on the end of Long Island, which was my dream home. My mother was still alive, and we saw her quite often at this time. I'm sorry my dad wasn't; he never would have imagined that he would have a son who could live in such a gorgeous place. We also had a home in West Palm Beach, Florida.

During this time, I started to dress as a woman at Thanksgiving and Christmas. It was just Akiko and myself, and I would prepare everything. I would set the table, arrange the menu, cook the food, and prepare a special dessert. I would dress appropriately for the occasion, and my persona for the day was like Martha Stewart. I loved doing it, and it made for an easy holiday for Akiko. The only issue was that my relatives didn't understand why I would never visit them on Thanksgiving or Christmas Day. That was my time. Naturally, I was nervous about my feminine appearance, but when I looked at the pictures my wife took of the holidays, I realized that I didn't look too bad. I still thought, secretly, "Maybe I can pull this off."

At this time, I was also doing a lot of traveling. I was on the road more than forty weeks a year, lecturing around the world. I spent significant time in airports, and it was then that I found myself people watching. But I wasn't evaluating the women as a man would. I judged them according to what they were wearing, making note of what I found attractive and what styles didn't work. Also, anytime I would go back to Japan with my wife, I would buy all the new half magazines I could find. Then I would hide them in my suitcase when going back to the States. Akiko knew that, and I guess she thought that I would somehow grow out of my habits.

What I was really doing at the time was compartmentalizing my feelings. By compartmentalizing them, I was able to just lead my life, but I was kind of on autopilot. I had gained a fair amount of weight because, as is typical in relationships with trans individuals who have not yet come to terms with their real gender, the last eighteen years of my marriage were asexual. My marriage was platonic, almost like a business relationship. I just couldn't have sex with a woman as a man; it just didn't seem right. On the other hand, I was doing a job I loved: I was creating products, I was lecturing, I was teaching, I was making a very good income. However, I always fought to suppress my thoughts about changing gender. I thought that by dressing like a woman just a few times a year, somehow I could get along.

In Florida, our home was part of a country club, and I played a lot of tennis. My wife was an excellent tennis player. I played tennis with her and the other women, wishing that I were wearing a women's tennis outfit instead of a T-shirt and men's shorts. I managed to indulge my feminine side a tiny bit, and I thought that was enough. I grew out my hair, so I looked more like an artist or a musician than an endodontist, and I continued to wear clear nail polish and shave my body. I also occasionally wore women's underwear and pushed the boundaries with women's shorts and warm-up suits. I tried to incorporate as much of a feminine mind-set into my daily life as possible without giving myself away.

However, everything changed in May 2011, two weeks before my annual specialty conference, when I was diagnosed with a squamous cell cancer on the back of my right hand. This was a big wake-up call, and awareness of my mortality set in. Having a health issue be the trigger for a sudden change of heart is very common with older trans people who wait to transition, but I didn't know that at the time, and when confronted with the possibility of death, I thought, "Oh my God, I have to get this [the transition] done before I die." Fortunately, my squamous cell cancer was a dermatological cancer, and dermatological cancers can be either melanoma (bad) or non-melanoma (not as bad). Squamous cell skin cancer is a non-melanoma cancer, meaning that yes, it theoretically can metastasize, but generally does only in severely immunocompromised people. But in my world of the oral cavity, a squamous cell cancer is an onerous diagnosis. The five-year survival rate, especially with a recurrence, is very low. Consequently, when I was diagnosed with a squamous cell cancer, even though mine wasn't in my mouth, mortality hit me like a ton of bricks. Game over! I had to change gender before it was too late.

3 · MY FIRST STEP

Facial Feminization Surgery

LIFE AFTER CANCER DIAGNOSIS

As I mentioned before, with mature individuals who wish to change gender, it is very common for a trigger event to put the wheels in motion. It could be the death of a spouse, a car accident, or surviving cancer. Some people interpret a trigger event as a traumatic episode that leads to an emotional, rather than a rational, decision to change one's gender. While some patients may experience such a response, I don't wholly support that belief. I do think that an emotional, life-changing trigger may be a catalyst for change for mature transitioners, but I believe that there is a physiological basis for gender dysphoria as well, and I fully expect to see more research confirming this fact in the future.

In my case, after my squamous cell cancer diagnosis in May 2011, I knew that I had to transition before I died. I simply could not imagine dying as a man; it just seemed so wrong! Fortunately, my cancer was removed and my prognosis was favorable, so I got another chance to finally make the switch.

Throughout this period, Akiko was very understanding and supportive. I did not share with her my long-term intentions other than my desire to lose weight. We were able to enjoy a nice summer without contention, but by autumn 2011, I knew I had to take other preparatory steps. The first thing I did was to begin facial electrolysis, which is an expensive, painful procedure. It was very challenging trying to explain this to my wife. Why would a man want to begin facial electrolysis? I gave a lame excuse about wanting better skin, and whether she believed this or not, she didn't protest too much.

Even though I had lost sixty-five pounds and had begun facial electrolysis, I still had not discussed my gender changing intentions with Akiko. Looking back now, this was, of course, a big mistake. But transitioning is so damn hard to do as a mature man. It isn't easy for anyone to admit to their families and loved ones that they are not the person everyone thinks they are, but I personally think younger people and transgender men generally have an easier time breaking the news. For older men, transitioning to be women, this can be very difficult, as there is just so more baggage when you're older. There is massive embarrassment and shame when you finally admit what you truly want to the people you love. There is also a lot of guilt, because you see yourself as being completely selfish, especially if they see you as the patriarch or breadwinner of the family. Looking back, I can definitely say that whether it is difficult or not doesn't matter. What *is* most important is that your spouse needs to be informed fairly early in the game if you hope to have any support throughout the lengthy and painful transition process. It's just being fair; remember: your transition affects many people!

While my personal life was changing, I continued to run my business and lecture on endodontics all over the country. Colleagues remarked how healthy I looked because I had lost weight and seemed to be in an upbeat mood. No one suspected anything unusual.

What kept me pushing forward was this intense desire to finally change gender. I have since witnessed this in many gender dysphoric people—the desire to change sex becomes so strong it borders on compulsion. It gets even more intense when one begins cross-hormonal therapy. However, at this point in my story, I was not taking any hormones, as I did not want to risk having Akiko discover my cache of pills. That would have let the cat out of the bag before I was ready. As long as I didn't take any hormones, she seemed okay with my behavior. However, I still incorporated certain feminine aspects into my daily routine—wearing some women's clothes and continuing to wear clear nail polish. Although these acts were minor efforts, they gave me great peace of mind.

What I want to stress again here, although I discuss it at length later in the book, is that you need to have a game plan to successfully transition. This is especially important for the mature individual, because you have so many relationships in place, both business and personal, that have been established for years. The fact that a mature man suddenly wants to change sex is not so easily digested by long-standing friends and family members. You need to have an idea of where you are going and how you plan to get there. Trust me on this.

GETTING TO CHESTNUT HILL

By October 2011, I had finally decided that I could not wait any longer and that I was going to transition. But instead of contacting a therapist or an endocrinologist, which is the recommended and smart way to do things, I chose instead to start my transition by contacting a plastic surgeon. I felt confident in my self-diagnosis from spending hundreds of hours in the medical libraries at Penn and Harvard researching gender identity disorder and gender dysphoria, and since I didn't need to rely on insurance to pay for my transition, I was free to approach it any way I wanted. My other reason for starting with my face was that I wanted to appear as much like a woman as I could, and I had to know if this was at all possible.

After doing some research, I made a phone call to the office of Dr. Jeffrey Spiegel in Chestnut Hill, Massachusetts, requesting a surgical consultation for facial feminization surgery (FFS). This first step took a lot of nerve because I suddenly realized that I was going down a path from which there was really no turning back. But I was somehow able to summon the courage, and I made an appointment with Dr. Spiegel for a surgical consultation. The appointment was set for November 5, 2011.

October came and went, and I returned to Long Island before leaving for Chestnut Hill, which is near Boston. I needed to determine how I was going to dress and present myself at the consultation appointment. One of the first things I decided to do was to go to a beauty salon on Long Island called Frasada. I had become a regular customer there, and they were, in actuality, my only emotional support system at the time, because I did not feel I could discuss any of my transition plans with Akiko. In particular, there were two women who worked at Frasada who were completely understanding of my situation. In fact, Claudia, the salon owner, sent me a Christmas card that year, wherein she wrote, "You are my hero." I didn't necessarily agree with that and told her so, but she said, "You're absolutely my hero for being true to yourself." Anyway, the people at Frasada were wonderful, so I decided that the day before my consultation, I was going to have my hair styled, have my nails done, and even have a couple of false eyelashes placed. These were all first-time events for me. So, I did have all that work done, and then I drove back to Old Field, where we lived. What made this easier for me was that at this time, Akiko was staying in our house in Florida, so I could come back from the salon looking a bit feminine without too much concern other than avoiding my neighbors.

I planned on taking the 7:00 P.M. ferry from Port Jefferson on Long Island over to Bridgeport, Connecticut, and then driving up to Chestnut Hill. I would stay in a hotel for the night, and the next morning, I would drive over to Dr. Spiegel's practice. I had an appointment at nine o'clock, and following the appointment, I would drive back down to Bridgeport and take the ferry across to Long Island. But one of the problems I was still wrestling with was how to dress when going up to Boston and checking into the hotel. In my heart, I had fully committed to the transition, finally, but to the outside world, I was still a man, and I was worried about harassment. Since it was November and cold, I could wear gloves, so people wouldn't see my nail polish. I also decided that I should go to the bathroom before I got on the ferry. Bathroom access was going to be an issue. I finally decided to dress androgynously, which to me meant that I had on just a little bit of lipstick. I wore two stud earrings and a nice pair of ladies' corduroys. A unisex type of sweater and a coat completed my ensemble.

I proceeded to the ferryboat. Fortunately, I had made an advance reservation, so I just needed to sign my credit card at the bursar's office. I did so with my gloves on. Of course, I was deathly afraid that I was going to see somebody I knew—or worse yet, that somebody I knew would see me! But on the Port Jefferson ferry, you are able to stay in your car down below, unlike on some other ferries. So, once I actually paid for my ticket, I went below deck and sat in my car. Everything was going swimmingly. I disembarked at Bridgeport and continued to drive up Route 95, all the way into Boston and eventually into the Chestnut Hill area. The hotel in which I was planning to stay was the Marriott Courtyard, but it was in a confusing section of town. I got up to Chestnut Hill around 10:15 P.M., and I had enormous trouble finding the hotel. Since Boston is a city of one-way streets, the next thing I knew, I was completely lost. I had lived in Boston for a number of years, and now here I was, totally lost! To make matters worse, I was getting more upset by the minute, practically panicking. I kept thinking, "I am a doctor;

this cannot be happening! I never panic!" Yet here I was, trying to look like a woman for the first time in public, and I couldn't find the damn hotel. I was so upset that I couldn't even set my GPS, which I really didn't know how to operate anyway. I tried to calm myself down and stop hyperventilating. Finally, after about an hour or so of roaming around lost, at around 11:30 at night, I rolled down my window and, in my most feminine voice, asked a passerby where the hotel was. He gave me a convoluted description, but then pointed out where it was. I realized I could get there more quickly going up a one-way street in the wrong direction. But I also realized this guy didn't seem to be responding in a strange way to me, which also calmed me down some. I gave a quick glance, and there were no cars coming. So, I drove quickly up the one-way street the wrong way and reached the hotel's parking garage. My plan was quite simple. I would just go upstairs, sneak into the lobby, register, and then go to my room.

I went upstairs, and as I walked into the lobby to register, I saw that it was packed! It was totally jammed with young men and women. I didn't realize it until later, but that was the night of the Notre Dame–Boston College football game. I went to the lobby desk to check in, and when I did, I had to take off my gloves. So there I was, with my painted nails, checking in, and there's a young man behind the counter. I decided that I would try to pass myself off as a little Goth, and that maybe he wouldn't think that was too weird. I shouldn't have worried because he couldn't have cared less. Following registration, I made a beeline to the elevator and went up to my room.

The next morning, I woke up, took a shower, and then had to decide what I was going to wear. When I'd packed, I put in three different styles of clothes, so that I would have some options depending on the situation I found myself in and how safe I felt. I'd packed some chinos and a man's style button-down shirt and sweater, in case I had to protect myself by dressing as a man. I'd packed another, more androgynous outfit as a middle option. As a third option, I'd packed a beautiful pair of women's black slacks, with a cashmere black sweater and a pair of two-inch heels.

I can still remember as if it were yesterday looking into the suitcase. I had gotten out of the shower, and since my electrolysis wasn't yet complete, I had shaved and applied a little bit of light makeup. I thought I looked pretty good. But in terms of actually putting on the clothes, I still had a dilemma. What should I wear? I went back and forth about it. And then I had a moment when I said to myself, "If you don't do it now, you're never getting out of the suitcase." I didn't think about my situation as getting out of the closet or being in the closet. I had never thought about my life with reference to that term. But when I thought about being my authentic self, the suitcase metaphor seemed to fit—either I would wear my true gender proudly, or it would live forever packed away, and I'd already tried that. So, I went ahead and opted for the women's slacks and the black cashmere sweater, along with the two-inch heels.

As I walked out of my hotel room into the hallway, I had an epiphany. It was like that cheesy stuff you see on TV where somebody dies and then they go to heaven and there is a golden staircase leading up into the clouds. I walked out of the room and felt something akin to a golden aura in front of me. I realize this was imagined, but I had a definite sense of enlightenment, a sense of freedom that I wasn't prepared for. I had never stepped out of my house dressed as a woman. Never! As I walked out into the hallway, there was this incredible feeling, like I was ascending my own golden staircase. It was startling and a bit unnerving.

THAT FIRST TERRIFYING APPOINTMENT

Having checked out on the television set inside the hotel room, I went down in the elevator to the lobby and proceeded to the parking lot in the basement. I can still vividly remember walking across that parking lot in Chestnut Hill with my heels clicking, thinking, "Oh my God, this is what I've been thinking about for so many years. I'm walking, and my heels are clicking like a woman's." It was a lot to process. I went across the parking lot to my car, and I proceeded to drive, heels and all, over to Dr. Spiegel's office. I parked, walked to the office building, and checked in at the doctor's office. Kate, a young woman in her twenties, was working at the desk. I introduced myself, checked in, and proceeded to take off my coat and gloves. As I did so, she complimented me on my nail color. Immediately, I felt reassured that my journey was off to a good start.

I had been sitting in the waiting room for only a few minutes when another young woman, Katie, ushered me into an exam room and asked me to sit down in a chair. She then left and closed the door. That's when the panic set in. It had been extremely difficult for me to go out in public dressed as a woman for the first time. Until you have an experience like that, you have no idea what courage it takes. It is absolutely terrifying. I have a friend who describes it like the feeling of deliberately jumping off a cliff. However you want to describe it, to me it was sheer terror. And as I was sitting there, with the door closed, I started to panic, thinking, "Oh my God, she's calling the police. They're calling security. Who am I kidding? I can't pass as a woman. What do I think I'm doing here? I can't pull this off." I was getting so upset that I realized I was going to faint. And then I thought, "I'm going to faint and pass out. This is going to be mortifying." But I looked down at the chair I was sitting in and realized that it was like a dental chair and that I could tilt it back a little bit. And then over in the corner of the office I saw a sink with a cup sitting next to it. I immediately went over to the sink to inspect the cup. I didn't care who had drunk from the cup. I didn't care what had previously been in the cup. I needed to have a glass of water! I was perspiring, but I wiped off the sweat and got back into the chair. I leaned back and, thank God, didn't pass out. I cannot imagine ever again in my life experiencing more terror than I did at that moment.

I sat in the chair trying to relax for what seemed like an eternity but, in reality, was probably only ten or fifteen minutes. The young woman from earlier, Katie, then came back in. She said, "You know, the first thing I have to say is that you look terrific." She continued, "You understand the concept of femininity all the way from the way your hair is done down to your nails." This, of course, was very reassuring to hear, even if she said it to all the patients to put them at ease. She continued, "There is, however, one thing that we need to address before we get started."

I said, "Uh-oh, what's that?"

She pointed to her clipboard and said, "This is your medical history. You've got a name here on this sheet that we cannot call you by. Obviously, you have been doing this for years [meaning dressing as a woman]. What's the name that you use?" I didn't have the nerve to tell her that this was the first time I had ever gone out dressed as a woman. I didn't want to seem like a complete idiot or totally unprepared. So, in my most nonplussed manner, I tried to come up with a name very quickly. And the name I came up with was my grandmother's. As I previously mentioned, she had asked me on multiple occasions if I ever wanted to be a girl, and because of that, I felt a special affinity for her. She seemed to see the true me when no one else did. So when Katie asked me what name I used, the name that came to my mind was Anne McCormick.

I said to Katie, "Anne."

She repeated, "Anne?"

I said, "Yes, Anne, or you can call me Annie." That's what we called my grandmother, Grandma Annie. And you know what? Annie works for me, and it's age appropriate. It's not Brittany or Tiffany or Caitlyn. It's Annie.

And Katie said, "Well, Dr. Spiegel will be with you shortly."

I felt so much relief that I had gotten this far into the appointment and had gotten past the initial terror. A few minutes later, Dr. Spiegel came in, and I was just blown away. I have known many surgeons, as well as many successful doctors in the medical and dental fields. In fact, I had been one of them. But I was struck by Dr. Spiegel's compassion, understanding, and professionalism. I talked to him, and he actually listened. We talked at length about what "we" were trying to achieve, as if we were already a team. And since I had familiarized myself with all the different options before my appointment, we were able to talk those over. He was completely understanding of my personal situation with my wife and seemed genuinely interested in my current business and my professional background. I told him that I was involved in endodontics and that I was a recognized name in my field. I found myself being very comfortable sharing my history, my current status, and my aspirations with Dr. Spiegel.

Dr. Ousterhout, in San Francisco, was the doctor who created and refined the art of facial feminization. Dr. O, as he was called, was well known for giving his patients "the works," which he would do in marathon appointments. However, at my age, I was a little concerned about the amount of time needed under anesthesia for these types of marathon sessions. Dr. Spiegel suggested I could do the surgery in two appointments. Yes, there was a little more money involved in terms of anesthesia and other surgical costs, but this was something I felt I had to do, as I was trying to transition in a manner that was staged and deliberate, in order to cause minimal collateral damage to both my personal life and my business. Therefore, for the first facial feminization surgery session, we decided to do only a few procedures—a neck lift; a blepharoplasty, which is removing the fatty tissue from the eyelids; and malar implants (cheek implants). Personally, I think a neck lift is the most dramatic facial procedure a person could have done, male or female. Not only does it take away the saggy neck skin below your chin, but it gives you a much sharper profile. It also makes you look a lot younger. I figured I could pass that off to nosy inquirers as just wanting to look more youthful. The lower bleph is kind of the same thing. Men and women both have that done, because by removing some of that fatty tissue, you remove that tired, haggard look that so many people get as they age. A blepharoplasty will definitely make you look younger. In fact, many of the procedures that are done to make you look more feminine also make you look younger, and procedures that make you look younger also make a guy look a little more feminine.

One change I couldn't just pass off as an anti-aging procedure was the introduction of the cheek implants. I knew they would create a distinctively different look for my face. I personally like that contoured look. I didn't want to have a round, cherubic appearance. So, we decided on those three procedures for the first visit.

While I was pleased with the progress I was making in terms of planning my surgery, I was still in a quandary concerning emotional support. A support person is recommended, although not mandatory, when one undergoes FFS. My problem was that Akiko was not interested in joining me at the hospital. I think she felt as though she was losing her husband. I had not shared my true intentions with any friends or colleagues, although I did mention to a few that I was having some procedures done to "look younger."

ANNIE'S FIRST FACIAL FEMINIZATION SURGERY

My first surgery was scheduled for January 2012 at Boston Medical Center. When working with Dr. Spiegel, a patient has the option of setting up the appointment as an outpatient visit, going to a hotel immediately afterward and spending eight days recuperating there, as long as everything goes well, after which Dr. Spiegel dismisses you and you can go home. So, I made a reservation with the hotel that Dr. Spiegel had an arrangement with, and the hotel staff and their manager, Lauren, ended up being so incredible and understanding that I was happy I had chosen that option. Since the doctor worked with them a lot, they knew exactly how to treat those patrons who were there for extended-stay recoveries, and I will never forget their kindness.

That January, I checked in at the hotel the night before the procedure. The next morning, I got up, followed all the pre-op instructions, and took a taxi to Boston Medical Center. I checked in early at the hospital, did all the required paperwork, and eventually got my tags and was taken upstairs to the operating room. As I lay on the gurney, some medical students came by to investigate my case, because Boston Medical Center is a training institution. In fact, it now has an entire Center for Transgender Medicine and Surgery. As people came by, nobody mis-gendered me or called me by my previous name, Ken; not one person. Everyone was very pleasant. They seemed to know about my background as an endodontist as well.

Eventually, I was prepared for surgery. The IV was started, and that was it. When I woke up, I was not doing well in the recovery area, so they decided that I should spend the night in the hospital. Because of all the athletics I've done over the years, I have a very low heart rate—my resting heart rate is about thirty-eight beats per minute, which is in the range of marked bradycardia. As a result, it takes me a little more time to come out of anesthesia. I was in no shape to go back to the hotel. After having this experience, I would strongly recommend that anyone having facial feminization surgery spend the first night in the hospital, if you can, just in case something happens and you need care immediately. I don't remember too much about that night because I wasn't planning on being there, but I do remember having a Barton's bandage around my head. That's the one that looks like the bandage from the film *The Invisible Man*. The next morning, I woke up, and Dr. Spiegel's surgical fellow was there to check on me. Dr. Spiegel runs an FFS fellowship program, in which he helps train the next generation of surgeons in facial feminization surgery. As part of their training, they help the doctor during and after his surgeries. Finally, I got permission to leave the hospital and go back to the hotel.

I entered the hotel, went up to my room, and collapsed on the bed, just me, all alone. As I mentioned before, most people have somebody with them, encouraging them and making sure they're okay when they go through major surgery. I had no one. Instead, I had a little stuffed moose that I'd bought at Filene's and to whom I'd given a pair of Ray-Ban sunglasses and the name Frenchy. In addition to Frenchy, there was another even smaller moose. These guys were in my room all the time, and that was my entire support system as I started my recovery period. I remember lying in bed, thinking, "What the hell did I ever do to piss off so many people such that here I am all bandaged up and my only support system is a stuffed moose!" In retrospect, if I hadn't been so paranoid about hiding my transition from everyone, perhaps I could have asked someone to be with me, but I really don't know who that could have been. I asked Akiko to come, but she had no interest.

FIRST RECOVERY

I took pictures of myself during my recovery stay at the hotel, some of which appear in this chapter. I looked like a pumpkin—there was a lot of swelling. I was black and blue under my eyes from the blepharoplasty. I also had some swelling and bruising as a result of the cheek implants. I was temporarily numb on one side of my face, from the lip area up to my cheek. This paresthesia was coming from the incision made in the back of my mouth, where the cheek implant had been placed.

I just lay on my bed for days and tried to make myself comfortable. Amazingly, there wasn't a tremendous amount of pain. As for the pain that *was* present, I didn't take any medication to relieve it. For me, the pain was a reminder of how important this step was. It made me think, "This is what you asked for." I convinced myself to hang in there the best I could. I listened to music and watched television. These distractions, however, weren't so helpful. It would have been so nice to have had someone to talk with, but that wasn't to be. I think what got me through the experience was the fact that I had made this commitment. By day four I was getting a little antsy being cooped up in the hotel room all day and night by myself, so I decided to walk over to the nearby Italian section of Boston, the North End. I went to my favorite Italian coffee shop, Caffé Vittoria, on Hanover Street. I walked in and sat down, and this brassy waitress came up to me and said, "Excuse me, honey, but you look like you've been in a fight—and you lost."

I said to this waitress in my most feminine voice, "I'll have a cappuccino and a slice of your fabulous rum cake." She brought me the cappuccino and the rum cake, and I even took a picture of that.

At days five and six, I looked like somebody from *Planet of the Apes*. But I was actually starting to feel a little bit better, even though I now had a significant amount of bruising, or what we professionally call ecchymosis. It looked bad, but I was not in a tremendous amount of discomfort. I would go down to the hotel restaurant in the morning to eat breakfast. I wasn't embarrassed about the bruising because there were other people at the hotel who had also had surgical procedures. So I would simply go down and eat, and people didn't stare at me, for which I was very grateful. I just felt that things were healing. After days five and six, and especially during days seven and eight, my appearance changed dramatically. At the seven-day point, I looked beat up, but now, for the first time in my life, I looked like a beat-up woman. I still

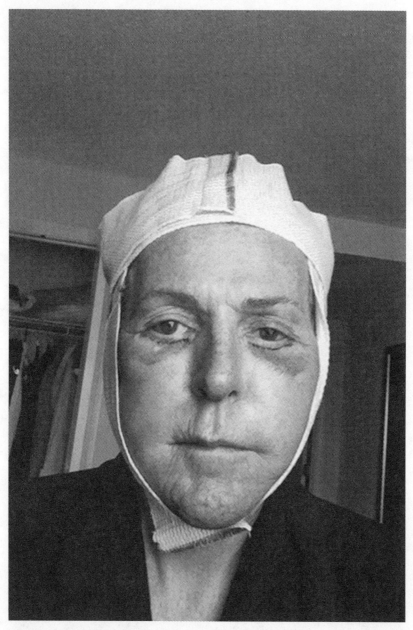

FIGURE 16. Day 3 post-op FFS, Boston, MA, 2012

Day 3 back at the Residence Inn Hotel in Boston. I am black and blue under the eyes as a result of the blepharoplasty, and I have some temporary numbness on my right side as a result of the incision for the malar implant. Not so much pain, but a general discomfort and feeling tired.

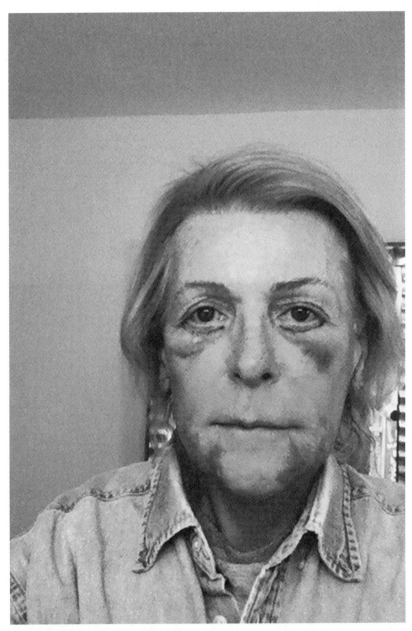

FIGURE 17. Day 5 post-op FFS, Boston, MA, 2012
At day 5, I had a *Planet of the Apes* look but actually felt pretty good. Was starting to feel like myself again.

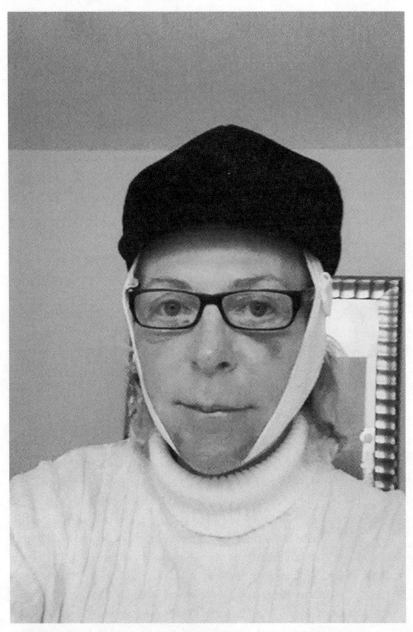

FIGURE 18. Day 8 post-op FFS, Boston, MA, 2012

By day 8, I looked beat up, but like a beat-up *woman*. It is quite stunning how quickly one heals from properly done FFS. I was beginning to feel very positive, and Dr. Spiegel answered all my questions.

had numbness on the side of my lip going up toward my cheek, but oh, I looked like a woman! At day eight, I had a follow-up appointment with Dr. Spiegel. I drove myself over to Chestnut Hill, and Dr. Spiegel examined me. He reassured me that my numbness would go away, and he had me do different types of lip movements to make sure that the numbness was nothing more significant than a transient paresthesia. After the examination, I was free to return home to Long Island.

MY NEW APPEARANCE

While in Old Field for the next two weeks, I took a picture of myself in the guest quarters of my home. I was quite slender then and had on knee-high boots and a beret, and I sent the picture to a couple of people to gauge their reactions to my transformation. They all said, "Oh, you look so different!" My appearance was striking to some people because this was before the transgender explosion we have witnessed in this country, and they had never seen such a change.

This strong reaction was just in response to the minor facial feminization I'd had done, as I hadn't yet touched my forehead or my nose, the two major areas of facial feminization. The features of the face that are a dead giveaway to people that you are a guy are the forehead, with the orbital bossing that gives one a Neanderthal-like look above the eyebrows; a large nose, out of proportion with the rest of the features; and, of course, a prominent Adam's apple, or what is called the cricothyroid area. On my initial facial feminization surgery, because I was trying to be discreet, I didn't have any of those areas addressed. But as a testament to Dr. Spiegel's incredible skill, after just the neck lift, the blepharoplasty, and especially the cheek implants, I now had a decidedly feminine appearance. In fact, at the six-week point, I took a selfie that is now my favorite picture of myself of all time. I had come back from Frasada, where I had had my hair done, and I was in a flannel nightgown, getting ready for bed. In that picture, I look exactly how I had imagined I would look for so many years! I had become my mother. My mother had been a singer for NBC in her youth, and she had a picture in her room for years, which sadly is lost, of her with her hair up. I idolized that photo. After I took that picture in my hallway in Long Island of me in my flannel nightgown, I felt as though I had taken my rightful place in my matrilineal family tree.

FIGURE 19. Two weeks post-op FFS, Long Island, NY, 2012
Back at my home on Long Island, with this bohemian Edie Brickell thing going on.
My friends were completely stunned to see this picture. Actually, I sent it to only a few
people.

FIGURE 20. My favorite photo, with a strong resemblance to my mother
Five weeks post-op from my surgery, I had my hair done at Frasada Salon, and when
I returned home, I took a selfie. I was stunned. This was how I always imagined myself.
This picture remains my personal favorite even after all these years. It reminds me of a
beautiful picture of my mother that I used to idolize.

The biggest change in my personal relationships came after my first FFS procedure. The placement of the cheek implants changed my look considerably, and the combination of a different face and significant weight loss tipped off friends and associates that something was going on. And once I saw my female self emerging, I made the decision to fully transition—and to accomplish it as quickly as possible. Rushing headlong into the process is, of course, not recommended, as I had not yet given serious thought to therapy.

As a result of Dr. Spiegel's recommendation, I was able to enter the Transgender Medicine Program at Boston Medical Center. My primary-care physician was Dr. Jennifer Siegel, and I found her to be thorough, professional, and pleasant. A home run! Being a patient in the program allowed me to start on the path to eventual cross-sex hormone therapy while having someone monitor my lab values, such as my hormone levels and triglycerides. I cannot emphasize enough the need to have a good primary-care provider on your team who is well versed in transgender health care. This person may be a physician, a physician's assistant, or a nurse practitioner, but having them in your corner will help you translate and coordinate the work that other doctors are doing.

At this time, I began seeing a therapist on Long Island, who was a transsexual woman herself. She was both understanding and helpful as I worked through some of the mental and practical issues that I hadn't yet thought about, and eventually, she wrote one of my two obligatory letters for gender reassignment surgery. Support groups were not easy to find at the time on Long Island, so I didn't join one. That turned out to be a big mistake; I should have looked a little harder.

Since my appearance had changed so drastically already and because I was now on cross-sex hormone therapy, the urge to fully transition became even stronger. I tried to walk the thin line between male and female while simultaneously feeling out friends and associates. I purposely dropped hints about my transition and often used double entendres. Almost without exception, the hints were ignored or totally missed. I also hesitated in directly informing my spouse, hoping that somehow she would connect the dots. That was another big mistake. People may find it incredulous that someone making such a huge life change wouldn't inform their spouse, and they may find it equally amazing that the spouse wouldn't question the behavior. But unless you go through it yourself, you cannot imagine the difficulty in broaching the subject of a permanent transition with someone you realize may not understand or support that choice—a choice that radiates to the core of your existence and who you truly are. I thought that if I just left it alone, my wife would eventually figure it out and broach the subject with me, instead of the other way around.

April 1, 2012, was the worst day of my life, and nothing will ever match it. Meeting with my business associates to tell them my transition plans did not go well, and I was completely eviscerated by their reactions. Actually, I was reduced to tears. Not only was there the suggestion of me giving up my company in its entirety, but there was also the vague suggestion that the best thing for everyone would be if I committed suicide.

After spending a truly nightmarish five hours with these people, I returned home to find a worried, agitated spouse, who wanted to know why I looked so upset. When I told Akiko my nightmare story, she finally asked, "Well, what *are* your plans?" When I told her the truth, she also reacted very poorly, and it started all over again. She hurled all kinds of accusations, all kinds of hate. After two hours, I gave up trying to reason with her, completely exhausted. Finally, after seven full hours of recriminations and being told that I should give away my company and commit suicide, I retreated to my room, locked the door, and cried. It was so horrible. I cried for hours—out of frustration, self-pity, loneliness, and fear. I couldn't believe that everyone was deserting me all at once, and with such malice!

During this period, any crying on my own behalf engendered absolutely no sympathy from either my business associates or Akiko. In fact, it had the opposite effect. The hate and venom directed at me by all parties continued to be a shock. All the things I had done for people—like picking up restaurant tabs and entertaining friends—all the money I had made for my associates through my creativity and hard work, meant absolutely nothing. I was crushed by the response.

All my personal relationships were strained after that day in April. I tried to be smart and avoid any discussions about my gender change, but I had been identified as someone making a foolish "alternative-lifestyle" decision. In the aftermath of my revelation, Akiko and I separated for a while. I lived at the house on Long Island, while she stayed at the house in Florida. I was still lecturing and running my company on a day-to-day basis, but I knew that my future there was doomed. Everyone was turning against me. It all came to a head at the end of April 2012, after attending my specialty association's conference and the prestigious California Dental Association (CDA) meeting.

That year's American Association of Endodontists (AAE) conference was in Boston, so I felt obligated to attend, since it was so close. This was against the wishes of my business associates, who found my personal appearance strange and who thought it would generate too many uncomfortable questions. Most of the colleagues I saw at the meeting thought I looked good because of my weight loss, but there were a few people who speculated that I had cancer or AIDS.

After the AAE conference, I did one final meeting—the CDA in Anaheim. I was one of the featured speakers, and it was the last presentation given by Dr. Ken Koch. It was so strange giving that presentation, knowing it would be my last and that no one attending had any idea of my future plans. It went really well, and the people in attendance enjoyed it. Little did I know that this was to be the beginning of an ongoing dichotomy in my life. People who didn't know me previously enjoyed being in my company, whereas people who knew me as Ken were confused at my new appearance and were noncommittal in their support.

The summer came, and since Akiko was involved with a number of tennis leagues on Long Island, I moved down to our home in Florida. The separation was already solidifying. This was not a happy time for me. I was slowly realizing that changing gender was going to affect my professional and personal life more than I ever could have imagined. Looking back, I must've been in a state of denial, along with feeling a bit shell shocked. One mistake I made was not controlling the dialogue at this early stage of transition. For one of the few times in my life, I reacted too passively to events. However, I simply could not comprehend the vitriol directed at me from those I had worked with for so many years. Everything was collapsing—everything I had built, everything I had worked for. People seemed anxious to take over my business and take credit for everything I had created. It was like I was a wounded animal and they smelled blood. This sudden implosion of what had been a stable situation is a good example of why the attempted suicide rate for trans people is 41 percent. Even if trans people aren't generally happy pre-transition, at least it is a situation they know. Once those supports are removed, it is very hard to pick yourself up again. Thank God I never considered suicide as a real solution, even though some of my business associates suggested that I should.

The situation was just so sad. Here I was, doing something that I had contemplated my entire life, and I had zero support from those closest to me. The only support I had came from the wonderful ladies at the Frasada hair salon. My therapist suggested that my hormone use was to blame for my emotional reactions to this nonsense. Did I become more emotional because of the estrogen I was taking? I didn't think so, but I did find myself sharing my emotions more freely. As the nightmare of 2012 continued, I went ahead and booked a second round of FFS for November. If I was going to be ostracized, at least I was going to do what I wanted to do: become an attractive woman.

ANNIE'S SECOND FACIAL FEMINIZATION SURGERY

I scheduled the second facial feminization surgery for November 4, 2012, in Boston with Dr. Spiegel. The procedures that we decided to do included a replacement of the left cheek implant, because the first one had rolled in on itself, and a lip lift. This is where the surgeon makes an incision underneath the nose in order to reduce the length of the philtrum, the distance between the base of the nose and the upper lip. Men have a longer philtrum than women do, so for a trans woman, a lip lift is a great procedure. In addition to giving the face a more youthful and feminine appearance, the procedure can roll back the upper lip, giving the patient more exposed lip area.

I also had a hemangioma (a noncancerous growth of blood vessels) on my upper lip, and the surgical team wanted to remove that. In addition, I decided to have a rhinoplasty. I had a nice nose for a guy, but I wanted them to make it a little bit thinner and create a little bit of an upturn at the end, to make it seem a little more youthful. Finally, we decided to do some mandibular recontouring at the angle of the mandible. If you put your fingers at the back of your jaw, there is a kind of angle where the jaw comes out and then goes forward. That's the angle of the jaw, and men generally have a sharper, squarer angle, whereas women have a more rounded contour. So Dr. Spiegel was going to soften that angle and recontour the front of my jaw. Some surgeons will actually do a more involved procedure, where they slide the mandible back. I didn't need that. Basically, what I asked Dr. Spiegel to do was minor work. For a plastic surgeon, it's easier to just go in and blow everything away and start over on a blank canvas, but I wanted Dr. Spiegel to make me look like Ken Koch's sister. Of course, I never had a sister, but I wanted to look like what a sister of mine might possibly look like. I didn't want to have a face that looked like everybody else's; I wanted to have my own face. One thing I decided to wait on was basic forehead recontouring. I don't have a lot of frontal bossing; in fact, I have the kind of forehead that is similar to that of a number of female athletes—and being a female athlete is totally my vibe. I did consider it strongly, though, because forehead recontouring makes a dramatic change in your appearance. In retrospect, I probably should have gone ahead and had the forehead recontouring done at the same time as the rhinoplasty. When they do the forehead recontouring, the surgeon generally advances the scalp. At the time, my thinking was, "Well, let me just wait on that a bit, and if I decide down the road to have a facelift, I can do the recontouring in conjunction with that." At this point, I still haven't had a facelift. People don't seem to have any issues with my forehead. But since I give a lot of lectures, I always think about my forehead and wonder how it is being received. I go back and forth about it to this day.

So for the second facial feminization surgery, even without the forehead restructuring I was increasing the number of procedures being done. As subtle as each may have been, I wanted to have them all done at the same time, to finalize my facial appearance. They remembered me at the hospital when I checked in. But when I came out of the operating room, my experience was very different from that of my first visit. Now that I was prepared, I had planned on spending one night in the hospital after the procedure. As it turned out, I ended up spending an additional night there, because when I came out of the operating room, I was really swollen. I looked terrible, because Dr. Spiegel had done a lot of work at the same time. In fact, I was so swollen that I was having trouble sucking anything through a straw. So the nurses, who were amazing, crushed up my medication and put it into chilled applesauce, then took a spoon and basically forced it through my lips. My lips were so swollen that I couldn't even move them. But the chilled applesauce was wonderful, since my throat was quite dry from the anesthesia. I was very pleased to see that Dr. Nasseh—one of my ex-residents, whom I had always tried to mentor and whom I eventually chose to replace me as CEO and president of my company—had come to visit me in the hospital. In the stupor of my postoperative anesthesia and pain medication, I remember his presence on that very rainy, snowy night. I was very flattered that he had made the effort to come see me, and I will be forever grateful to him and proud that he had been my resident at Harvard.

After Dr. Nasseh left, I eventually fell asleep, and when I awoke the next morning, I realized that I was in a lot tougher shape than I had been after my first FFS. Dr. Spiegel's surgical fellow came by to check on me, and he was very reassuring about how everything came out. I got through the first two days in the hospital, and by the third day I was able to go back to my hotel room. I documented what I looked like again. When I took off the Barton's bandage, I saw that I was really beat up: my nose was bandaged, I was swollen around my lips, I had bloody sutures under my nose, I had a bandage over my left cheek, and my mandible was swollen. I wore the Barton's bandage for the next few days to help minimize the mandibular swelling, but I knew things were going to really swell up this time. By day four, I was really blown out in the bottom half of my face and had significant swelling, but this was totally expected. On day seven, I went over to see Dr. Spiegel for my post-op appointment. He reassured me that things were going to be fine. I had a little bit of numbness, but again, it was a transient type of paresthesia. Dr. Spiegel was pleased with the way things were healing.

What is amazing about plastic surgery is how quickly you recover. Three weeks later, I was back in Boston having dinner with Dr. Nasseh to thank him for visiting me in the hospital. It was remarkable how good I looked at the three-week point, even understanding that I was not going to see the full effects of the procedures until six months to a year after the surgery. That's one thing you have to realize with plastic surgery: You're not going to see any real results for at least six weeks; and if you want to see any significant results, you've got to give it easily three months. The changes become even more pronounced at six months, and many times it takes up to a full year before you see the final results. The thing is, it takes some time for everything to settle. This was especially true with my rhinoplasty, as it took some serious time for my nose to remodel itself. Once everything had settled, I was so pleased with how I looked that a few weeks later, I actually went back and had a medium-sized Permalip implant placed in my lower lip. This was at the ten-week point, at the end of January 2013. The Permalip is made of silicone, and they simply make two incisions in your mouth and then slide it through. The incisions are preceded by local anesthesia, which is the painful part of the procedure, as the doctors have to insert the anesthetic needles quite deep in order to nerve-block the anterior portion of your mouth. This now allows the surgeons to very painlessly go in and place the lower lip implant. Not only does the lower lip implant look terrific, but it feels totally natural.

In terms of my personal life after my second FFS procedure, things became less busy, as I sold most of my company stock to a larger dental corporation. I tried to keep my company, but it was to no avail, since my business partners were so adamant about not working with me any longer. Following the sale of the company, my life went in an entirely different direction. I had lost my business, and was in the process of losing my marriage.

Let me review my experience with facial feminization surgery. I didn't go for one long marathon visit. Instead, I split it up into two sessions: one that was about three and a half hours long, and one that was a bit longer, maybe four and a half hours. I split the sessions because I was trying to manage my transition in an orderly manner. I wanted to stagger the changes to my body to minimize their impact on my life. (I was actually trying to salvage both my marriage and my business relationships.) In retrospect, I think that was a big mistake. Managing your transition slowly doesn't make it any easier. If anything, it makes it more difficult, because it lengthens the amount of time you spend dealing with these changes. Because of my age, I was concerned about the amount of time I would be under anesthesia. That may have seemed a smart decision at the time, but after getting to know the facial feminization surgery world better, as well as Dr. Spiegel, I don't think it would have been a problem.

The only procedures that I regret not having done are forehead recontouring and scalp advancement. I was a little worried about just how few cases of forehead recontouring had been done at that time. You don't want to have your forehead shaved down so it's as thin as an eggshell. If you need a lot of forehead recontouring done, instead of shaving it, the surgeons will do an osteotomy, which is a technique in which they cut a section out of your forehead, recontour that bone, and then replace it. They attach it with titanium screws or bone cement, or a combination of the two, and the results are not only painless but incredible. Bone doesn't contain nerve fibers, so it's a painless procedure for the patient, with great predictability associated with it. The post-op complication rate is less than that with tonsillectomies. Dr. Spiegel has since become a world authority on this procedure. At the same time, the doctors can advance the scalp to fill in the widow's peak look that many trans women have. There has always been some concern by patients about where the surgeon makes the incision in the scalp and whether they will lose some of their hair grafts, if they have plug grafts. Most of the trans women I know have had hair plugs done, especially in the anterior of the head, to get a better hairline. But the loss of hair plugs is minimal with the scalp advancement. And if you do lose a couple of plugs with the scalp advancement, you can always have a hair transplant surgeon pop in a few more plugs later.

It is my opinion that some facial feminization surgery, especially for the older trans woman, is absolutely a must. Very young trans women can pass as cisgender women. But once you get to be thirty years old or older, testosterone has had enough of an effect on you that you are going to have very significant male characteristics. This is one of the arguments for the puberty suppression regimens that are being used with young trans children now, because it allows that person time to decide what they want in terms of gender. And, if they are boys, it also prevents them from having the strong masculine features that develop secondary to testosterone exposure. The three key areas for the male to female transgender woman to pay attention to are the forehead, the nose, and the cricothyroid area (Adam's apple). The only one of those three that I had addressed was the nose, and I just had that lightly recontoured. I had no need to have anything done with my Adam's apple. I may go back and have the combination forehead recontouring and scalp advancement done if I decide on a facelift as I age.

Another point about facial feminization surgery worth emphasizing is that many trans women think that once they have had FFS, they are done dealing with their face. Trust me, it's not the end; in fact, it's just the opposite. This is the beginning of the rest of your life, the beginning of you living your life as a woman. It's the beginning of you now having to follow a regimen of skin care maintenance, including using moisturizer and sunscreen, which many natal women follow in order to protect their skin. Even if you're not a particularly girly girl or a woman particularly concerned with aesthetics, you will have to maintain your surgery. Facial feminization surgery is analogous to periodontal surgery. If you have gum surgery and you don't maintain it through proper flossing and brushing, you're going to lose the results of the surgery—your gums are going to regress. It's the same thing with facial feminization surgery. If you have facial feminization surgery, especially at an advanced age, you're going to look younger and more feminine. But if you don't maintain it, the results are going to deteriorate—you're going to develop lines and creases. The big change in facial aesthetics over the last five years has been the move away from just filling in lines and creases to replacing lost volume (think Juvederm, Restylane, Perlane, and so on).

Unfortunately, most of this work is not covered by insurance, but some people are trying to change that. In fact, in Massachusetts, Harvard Pilgrim insurance now covers facial feminization procedures for transgender women. However, most insurance policies do not currently cover these procedures, so plastic surgery is something that you should plan for—and save for—accordingly.

In terms of which surgeon you should consult, there are methods you can use to evaluate different surgeons. Of course, I am biased. I think that Dr. Spiegel is absolutely terrific, but there are other good surgeons as well. You can even do an Internet search for surgeons in your area. When you're choosing a surgeon, you want someone who has experience. But you don't want someone whose only experience is doing plastic surgery with cisgender women. You want to choose a plastic surgeon that has experience in facial feminization surgeries on transgender women. This is important because of the significant skeletal differences between men and women.

In terms of passing and living your life as a woman, there's no comparison between the effect that facial feminization surgery has on your life and what gender reassignment surgery affords you. FFS may seem small potatoes when compared to the vastness of gender reassignment surgery, but facial feminization surgery has a far greater impact on your life because it affects how you present to the public. That's how people are going to see you in Home Depot. That's how they're going to see you at the supermarket. That's how your co-workers are going to see you. They are going to see your face, not what's below your waist and in your pants. So, do your research, make a thoughtful decision, and save your money accordingly. Going forward, you may see more medical centers doing training programs in facial feminization surgery. The doctors in those training programs not only have the luxury of time, meaning that they can do a good, thorough job, but are generally more inexpensive because they're still training. So, if money is an issue for you, that is something you may want to consider. Furthermore, the surgeons I know who are working in this area are very cognizant of the demands of facial feminization surgery—not just on their end, as surgeons, but, and more importantly, on the patients'. Dr. Spiegel was very attuned to the challenges I faced as a successful male transitioning into becoming a female. It helped so much that he had a great personality. There are many great surgeons who don't have a good personality or a good bedside manner. Not only is Dr. Spiegel a talented surgeon, but he has an incredibly compassionate manner. We could talk about things, and I felt comfortable that we were doing this together, as a team, rather than me simply being seen as a number. That is really important to keep in mind when choosing a facial plastic surgeon. Choose somebody who you are comfortable with, because FFS is something that's going to require maintenance. Your plastic surgery will need tweaking through the years, whether it's a facelift or blepharoplasty. You may want to have this done or that done in the future. Therefore, this is about establishing a relationship.

Finally, let me address the difference between getting facial feminization surgery that maintains your general appearance (looking like your sister) and getting FFS that makes you look totally different. I truly thought that if I presented to the world looking like Ken Koch's sister, my friends and family would receive me more positively, and that would make my transition easier. Unfortunately, that did not turn out to be the case. I think if anything, it was disconcerting and alarming to my friends, because they now seemed to regard me as a diminished version of Ken. If you are going in for facial feminization surgery and think that you would like to do it in a gradual or modest way (that you would like to maintain some of your looks), that's fine. Basically, I'm a happy girl; I'm thrilled with the way I look. But if you're doing it in such a manner because you think you're going to be better received by friends and relatives, that may not be the case. Just be prepared. In fact, I think if I had to do it again, the only change I would have made was to look more like an entirely new person rather than Ken Koch's sister.

4 · GENDER REASSIGNMENT SURGERY

Afटer my second facial feminization procedure, I eventually made my way back to West Palm Beach, and Akiko and I spent Thanksgiving and the Christmas holidays together. We were both trying to act like nothing out of the ordinary was happening. We had been sleeping in separate bedrooms for years, so that part wasn't unusual. Our marriage was a marriage of convenience more than anything else, and it had been for years. We played golf and tennis and tried to enjoy each other's company. I knew that I was working to somehow keep the relationship in place, but I did not know her intentions and was too nervous to ask. I knew that she did not want me to fully transition and that she was unhappy that I was taking hormones, but I did not know if she would demand a divorce if I proceeded with my plan. However, by this point, I was totally committed to a full gender change, so in January 2013, I decided to have a consultation with a gender reassignment surgeon. I chose a surgeon located in the Philadelphia area, which I thought would be more convenient, since I could travel there easily from our home on Long Island. However, out of respect for their privacy, I will not name this particular surgeon in the story that follows.

THE SURGICAL CONSULTATION

Before the surgery consultation, I think Akiko still held out hope that I would somehow reverse course and not go forward with my transition.

Consequently, she agreed to accompany me to the surgeon for the consult, and we took a road trip down to Pennsylvania and stayed in a motel. The next morning, I went over to the office for my consultation. After checking in, I was ushered into a consultation room. It wasn't long before the doctor came in. We talked over what I was looking for, and she asked me why I was there. By the end, I felt more secure. I was impressed with the doctor's thoroughness. At this point, I didn't know how many people this particular surgeon had seen during the course of her career who were around my age, but I knew that I was probably at the bottom of the curve. Finally, I had to disrobe and let the doctor check out the goods. The exam was conducted in a professional manner. She told me, "Annie, you are an excellent candidate. I have no problem doing the surgery. When would you like to have this done?"

Very cavalierly, I said, "How about tomorrow morning at 7:30?"

We both laughed, and the surgeon said, "Well, I know you've waited a long time for this. But here's the problem. I'm booked for nine months."

I said, "Nine months! That's incredible. Let me tell you something, I think I am an absolutely perfect candidate for a cancellation. I've got all the paperwork done, the letters from my therapist—everything I need. Also, I'm in great shape for somebody my age." The surgeon agreed. I continued, "I'm retired (which is how I was characterizing my ignominious ouster from my company), so I have unlimited time. I'm available anytime, and—perhaps most important of all—I have the resources. I can write a check right now."

The surgeon said, "Right, you are a great candidate for a cancellation, but there's only one problem. I rarely get any cancellations for this procedure."

I said, "Really? Well, if you ever get one, please keep me on the list. I'm ready to go." In my mind, I had already made the decision to go with this doctor—that I didn't need to go see surgeon number two or surgeon number three. I thought this doctor fit the bill. In retrospect, making such a snap decision was a mistake. Anyone considering gender reassignment surgery should visit two or three surgeons and keep their options open. There are significant differences between surgeons as far as their philosophy and attitude toward patients, and if, like me, you jump at the first doctor you see, you may not be choosing the best situation for yourself.

It must have been maybe two or three minutes after this conversation when the doctor got paged to the front desk. When she came back, she said, "You are not going to believe what that was."

I said, "What?"

Laughing, she said, "I just got a cancellation for a surgery date. If you want it, it's yours."

I replied, "I'll take it! By the way, when is it?"

She answered, "In two and a half weeks." In two and a half weeks? Of course I would take it! The doctor then told me that if I didn't get all my paperwork done ahead of time, she wouldn't do the surgery. I said to myself, "I like that. It's a no-bullshit approach." So, I made the decision. I took the appointment.

As I was on my way out of the room, she called after me. "Wait, I have one final question. Those cheek bones. Are those yours, or did you have those put in?"

I smiled and said, "That's Jeff's work," meaning Dr. Spiegel, who by now I was on a first name basis with.

We both laughed, and the surgeon said, "They look good." I was pleased that my gender reassignment surgeon thought that my facial surgery looked good.

So, I had the date set. I made the appointment with the front desk, and I put down a deposit. I was on the books for surgery in less than three weeks! Then, the front desk receptionist gave me lots of paperwork to read and sign. I had to go back home and get all these letters from different people for my file. I was also going to have to go up to Boston to get some of this documentation from my primary-care people.

THE RIDE HOME AFTER THE CONSULT

After I was finished at the surgeon's office, I went back to the hotel and met my wife. Akiko asked, "How did it go?" I described the consultation to her in detail, and told her that there was a cancellation, and that I had the opportunity, if I wanted, to have the procedure done quickly. There was of course no response from my spouse, which I totally understood. By this time, I foolishly thought that we had both come to terms with what my gender reassignment meant for our relationship.

It was while driving back to Long Island that I said to her, "I think I'm going to go ahead and do it." I can still remember the exact stretch of road we were on when I mentioned this to her, and there was a pause, a long pause, and I realized that she wasn't happy with the way things were going. Obviously, she had been hoping that at some point I would somehow turn things around. But at this point, it would have been like turning around the *Titanic*, and I told her, "I am not turning around. I'm going forward with it. I am going to have the surgery."

It was a very awkward moment, and she said, "Well, if that's what you have to do, then that's what you have to do." I didn't want to dwell on what this meant for our marriage or talk about the surgery too much with Akiko, because I realized this was not going to be such an easy thing to discuss. Also, because I knew that I might need her to act as my escort for the procedure, I didn't want to antagonize her unnecessarily.

PRE-SURGERY

It makes sense that gender surgeons have a rule about staying someplace the night before surgery, so that you're rested and ready to go to the hospital early. The plan was that I would stay Sunday night at a hotel, go over Monday morning to the hospital, have the procedure done, and then stay in the hospital until Thursday, when I would be discharged. Everything was set, but I had to have an escort in order to be discharged, and unfortunately, my wife was the only person available to act as an escort. I had asked a few close friends to go with me, and even my brother, but no one was able to make the time, so other than just hiring help, the only recourse I had was to ask Akiko to act as my escort. Fortunately, she agreed to come with me. This was an incredibly difficult thing to ask of her. In hindsight, I was selfishly thinking only about my upcoming surgery, not about what she might have been feeling. And how stupid of me not to have gotten Akiko her own room! I cannot believe how completely blind I was to the insensitivity of having her there. I should have just hired a nurse as an escort. My actions were so unfair to my wife, but I do appreciate the fact that she agreed to come anyway.

That night in our hotel room, I took a picture of myself as I went through the requisite pre-surgery protocol and thought, "This is the last picture of Ken." I didn't feel upset; I didn't cry. Akiko was also very stoic—the Japanese are good at that. I was actually very composed when we went to bed. I got some sleep, and then got up early the next morning because I had to be at the hospital at 5:30. The entire process was surreal. I was going about my business like it was routine, yet I was completely changing my life. I didn't

FIGURE 21. Morning of my GRS, March 25, 2013

Last picture of Ken Koch before I walked into the hospital for my GRS procedure. I like this picture because I think it is a very feminine pose, and I look relaxed, as if thinking, "Finally, after all these years of thinking about this, I am actually going to have this procedure!"

realize it at the time, but that morning it was like I was killing Ken and giving birth to Anne. That is a lot to process.

Akiko and I checked out of the hotel and drove over to the hospital. The day before, we had made a test run to make sure that we wouldn't be late or get lost. As it turned out, that was a good idea because, low and behold, even though it was March 25, 2013, it was snowing. I was so glad that we knew where we were going.

Eventually, we reached the hospital, and it too became part of the surreal situation. I asked Akiko to take a picture of me standing outside the hospital. I love that picture, as it is truly the last picture of me as Ken. But it's an image that I think is really feminine, particularly in how I'm standing there, holding my medical records. Then I entered the hospital and checked in with the front desk. Eventually, I had to leave Akiko, and it was the last time she'd ever see her spouse as Ken. Think about that. It is not so easy to talk about, even now. The only reason that I wasn't more emotional at the time was that I didn't know what the future would hold.

I was put on a gurney and left to wait with a warm blanket until my surgeon arrived. I have been in lots of operating rooms and have done a fair amount of surgery myself, so I understand the procedure very well. The anesthesia people and my surgeon went over a few details before they started. They were getting ready to start an IV line with a sedative and were preparing to wheel me in when I gave my surgeon a thumbs-up, like we used to give to air force pilots before they took off.

THE SURGERY ITSELF

Performing male-to-female gender reassignment surgery is much easier than performing a phalloplasty on transgender men. What is remarkable is that most of the original tissue is recycled and repositioned. The only parts discarded are the testes and the erectile material from the penis. The surgery begins with an incision in the scrotal tissue and the removal of the testes. A circular incision is made behind the glans penis, and the penile tissue is essentially rolled down along its shaft, and its components are dissected out. Erectile tissue is discarded, and the glans penis is maintained, along with the nerve that runs along the length of the shaft. Great care is taken to prevent damaging this nerve, as the glans penis (after being greatly reduced in size) along with this nerve will ensure a sensate neo-clitoris. The urethra is severed and repositioned, and the neo-vagina is constructed from inverted penile tissue sutured to scrotal tissue that has had its hair follicles removed. An assistant does a follicle scrape during surgery, but genital electrolysis is usually required before surgery. The labia minora are constructed from penile tissue, while the labia majora are created from scrotal tissue. Packing is placed into the new vagina, a catheter is inserted, and the wound area is dressed with gauze. The usual time required for this surgery is three to four hours, but time can vary widely based on the surgeon.

After giving the thumbs-up to my surgeon, I was wheeled into the operating room, and all I remember after that was sliding off the gurney onto the operating table. I passed out, and the next thing I knew, I was waking up, and my wife was speaking to me: "Annie, wake up. Annie, wake up! It's finished."

I was stunned. "It's already over?" I couldn't believe it. It had taken only two hours and twenty minutes. But while I had no memory of anything that had happened during the surgery, I cannot imagine what it was like for my wife to be sitting there for two and a half hours. I am certain that her mind kept revisiting all the changes that were taking place. It must have been a torturous time for her.

Eventually I was wheeled from the recovery room to my hospital room. I quickly realized that I was on my back and couldn't move—and that I was going to be like that for the next three days. The surgeons place packing, which is basically wrapped gauze or a surgical stent shaped like a dilator, inside your neo-vagina, and it is sutured into both your thighs and into your buttocks. They purposefully make sure nothing moves. If you even think about moving, it hurts like hell. This is really critical, because any movement by the patient may dislodge the stent and possibly jeopardize the skin grafts from healing correctly. As a patient, you have a morphine drip to help control the pain, but I don't think I used it even once. I'm not really into taking narcotic pain medication. Instead, I just lay still; in truth, the most uncomfortable pain I felt was in my lower back from not moving or sitting up, not from the surgical site itself.

It is so difficult lying there on your back, unable to move, eating nothing but ice chips. You're like a flipped tortoise. Since my heart rate was so low, my surgeon did not prescribe a sleeping pill. That meant I was a little bit

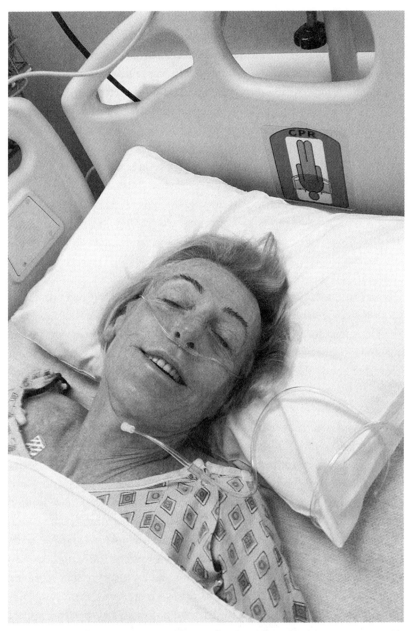

FIGURE 22. Immediate post-op picture, GRS, March 25, 2013
Photo taken immediately after surgery. I think I look peaceful and serene in this image.
I had my eyebrows and lashes tinted before the procedure so that I would look
presentable.

uncomfortable at night, particularly during the never-ending early-morning hours. You're lying there awake, and time seems to stop. At three o'clock you think, "I can't fall asleep, and I've been lying here for 25 minutes." But you take a look at the clock and it's only five after three. After that, you're lying there thinking that it must be twenty after three now, but it's only a quarter after three. That period between three and five in the morning never ends when you're in the hospital. Additionally, the staff wouldn't feed me until I was able to pass gas. We made jokes and laughed about that: farts are fun! But as I lay there, wanting to pass gas because I wanted to be able to eat something, I couldn't. So, I continued on the ice chips.

THE RECOVERY

That first day after my surgery, Tuesday, was a blur because I was recovering. Wednesday came, and I was getting a little anxious because I still could not pass gas. I don't remember exactly whether it was the second or third day after surgery when the nurses got me out of bed to walk. They were careful walking with me, but I felt surprisingly good, and it felt so great to be out of bed instead of flat on my back. By Thursday, when I was walking around, I was finally able to pass some gas, so the nurses gave me a little food to eat.

Thursday afternoon, the surgeon decided to discharge me. The physician's assistant had come by my room every day to check on me, but I only remember my surgeon coming by on the first day after surgery. I took that as a good sign, figuring she'd only bother coming by if there was a problem, but I very much appreciated the brief conversation we had the day she stopped in regarding the issue of a rectovaginal fistula, which can be a catastrophic complication for a vaginoplasty.

The possibility of getting a fistula had been my most serious concern about the surgery, but the surgeon reassured me: "You know that complication you were concerned about? Well, I checked the area a few times, and even used methylene blue [a disclosing dye], and everything is fine. It's not an issue." I was so relieved and pleased that the surgeon had used the methylene blue to confirm that there was no open connection between the rectum and the neovagina.

Since the hospital was discharging me, the nurse wanted to show me how to urinate with my new equipment. At this point, I still had the catheter tube in my urethra, and the nurse wanted to make certain that I knew how to use it. I went with the nurse into the bathroom, and she told me that I needed to be standing up, because there was now a tube sticking out where I used to have a penis. She gave me instructions on how to urinate: "Loosen the clamp, grab the rubber hose, and aim it into the toilet bowl." I couldn't help it, I started laughing.

"Wait a second, I just went through this entire procedure to be able to sit down when I pee, not to be standing up." We both had to laugh at the incongruity of it, but there I was. And I didn't have to practice anything—I'd been peeing that way for sixty-three years, thank you very much! Finally, I was able to get dressed and leave the hospital.

After my discharge, Akiko drove me from the hospital to a new hotel, which would act as my recovery room until the surgeon released me to travel home. Akiko was helpful and tried to be considerate, but she obviously wasn't happy. The reality of the situation and its finality were beginning to hit her. I felt sorry for her because I knew she felt abandoned and adrift. After my procedure, the surgeon spent very little time explaining things to her but spent significant time explaining things to the friends of another patient. That really bothered me, and I later asked my surgeon why she hadn't spent more time explaining things to my wife. She basically said, "Well, she's Japanese, and I didn't think she would understand." Akiko speaks and understands English very well, so that proved to be another frustrating interaction in this whole experience. I felt enormous guilt as we left the hospital. In many ways, I had just destroyed two lives. Akiko's life had been completely transformed by this surgery, but Ken's life was also over. I assume it is somewhat easier if you are not married, but transitioning isn't easy for anyone to do.

Regardless of her personal distress, Akiko drove me from the hospital to the hotel, and we checked in. The hotel staff was discreet, respectful, and helpful. The room we checked into had two beds: a large canopy bed, which Akiko would use, and one of those iron rollaway beds that was lower to the floor. That's where I would be.

I was happy to be out of the hospital, but my recovery period over the next week proved to be very difficult. It was painful and awkward to move around, and it was even more difficult to face Akiko. Regardless, I was very thankful for the assistance she provided. As time went on, however, her good nature changed. I remember precisely that the first full day I was in the hotel was

Good Friday, and the forsythias were blooming. I had the surgery on a Monday, which was actually Passover. I thought the religious coincidences were significant, because I was looking for signs or omens portending a positive outcome to my surgery. I didn't do much in the hotel those first days other than lie still and listen to music. I also watched a lot of music videos on my computer. What I did *not* do was talk much about the surgery with my spouse, which I now realize I should have done. I finally understood that she was angry, devastated at the changes this meant for her own life and very unhappy just being there. Looking back, it makes perfect sense that she felt that way, but because I was dealing with the completely absorbing task of healing my physical body, I completely missed her perspective. For the second time, I hadn't even thought of getting her a separate room. She hadn't objected to my proposal of sharing a room, so I thought it was acceptable. How utterly selfish that was. My willful blindness to her feelings just left her there to stew about everything. To be honest, I think we were both shell shocked about what had just happened—her more so than myself—and I was still in a lot of physical pain, too.

Finally, on Easter morning—a week after we had arrived at the first hotel and almost a week since the surgery—I went out. It felt so good. I said to Akiko, "Walk with me, please." It was such a sunny, warm spring day. "Just walk with me outside for about ten minutes." And she did that with me. I was rushing it by a day. I really shouldn't have been out walking until the next day, but I was very careful, and it felt great to be out. It also felt like I had been reborn. The flowers were in bloom, and it was a beautiful spring day in the Northeast. I did fine walking, and I didn't do any damage to my sutures. When we got back to the room, Akiko went down to the hotel restaurant to get us some real food for Easter. We ate in silence. Over the course of the next few days, things became tenser between us, and at one point I remember lying in my rollaway bed, freezing. As I've gotten older, I've become far more sensitive to the cold. Because I was freezing, I asked Akiko, "Could you please bring me the blanket that's over there in the closet?" I'd asked her to get me the blanket rather than getting it myself because at that point, any movement I made hurt. The sutures had been in my pelvic area for a number of days, and it was extremely painful to move. So, she got the blanket, and she brought it back . . . 90 percent of the way, and dropped it on a chair. It was just out of my reach, so I had to get up and get the blanket myself, and it hurt so much. That was such a mean thing for her to do. Months later, during our divorce proceedings, I told her, "You know, I just want to let you know that I didn't miss that time when you made me go and get the blanket in the hotel after my surgery. That was a terribly mean thing to do. It hurt me so much that you couldn't just help me when I really needed you. It was so disappointing." But at the time it made me think, "Why can't she just help me? She agreed to come. Why is she being so mean?" I still don't have the real answer for that.

THE BIG HOLE

After the Easter weekend, Akiko drove me back to the surgeon's office for my first post-op appointment. I was still bandaged down there, of course. While waiting for the doctor, I got on the scale. I had lost eleven pounds and was now 157 pounds. I hadn't been 157 pounds since junior high! I was indeed thin.

Soon, the physician's assistant came in and started preparing me for the examination. Then my surgeon came in and removed the entire dressing down below, took out the vaginal packing, and removed the catheter. That was when I finally had an opportunity to look down and see the results. I started panicking a bit, thinking, "What the hell did I do?" There was such a huge freaking hole where my genitals had been. It looked like I had stepped on a landmine. I kept wondering if I'd made a huge mistake. All gender reassignment surgeons must have experiences with their patients having this type of emotional response. They must see it all the time. But I was simply stunned at how I looked. The doctor reassured me that things were healing fine, and that yes, it is a shock now, but that things would get better. However, the first time you look down after a surgery such as this, there is no penis and testicles, and—even worse—there is no beautiful female genitalia either, because everything has been stretched out from the vaginal stent and surgical dressing. Certainly all the required anatomy is there, but the initial impression is that of a big hole. It was really a sobering experience. And then, of course, they explained to me what I was going to have to do to maintain the path that they had just created. An integral part of this upkeep involved showing me how to dilate and familiarizing me with my "new anatomy."

In order to maintain the openness of the new vagina, you have to dilate it by inserting a smooth, hard plastic rod called a dilator for a certain amount of time. And these are full-size dilators. They kind of look like a sex toy, but there is nothing exciting or sexy about them. They look like a bent dildo, and they come in graduated sizes. The doctor's staff explained to me in detail how to use the dilators and how often I had to use them. It is a very aggressive program, meaning that five times a day for twenty-five minutes each session I had to put the thing inside me. If you don't dilate, the body treats the neovagina like a wound and tries to heal itself—that is, close the wound. Since I am on the older side, my body, and more specifically my vagina, seems to have a little more tolerance. My vascularity down there isn't as robust as that of someone younger, so the wound doesn't try to close itself as aggressively as it might have otherwise. After this initial post-op visit, I returned to the hotel, and two days later there was another follow-up appointment. Eventually, the doctor cleared me to leave, and my wife drove us back to Long Island. While giving her directions on the way home, I gave her the wrong information, and we got lost. I said to Akiko, "Isn't this funny? In all the years I was a guy, I had a great sense of direction. I undergo sex change surgery, and now I've lost all sense of direction. But the good news is, I have no hesitation asking for help!"

IMPRESSIONS AND RECOVERY AFTER SURGERY

One of my first impressions after my genital surgery was that nothing had changed. When I woke up from the anesthesia, I thought that maybe I would feel different—like a different person. Nope. I woke up, and I didn't feel any different. I like to say that before I had the procedure, I didn't like soccer; and after the procedure, I still disliked soccer. It was reassuring that I was the same person I had always been, but surprising that I thought there might be a big change in how I felt about myself. But nothing about my personality changed. I did have a sense of having a phantom penis that first day and a half, but I was prepared for that. I kept thinking during that first day, "Do I still have a penis?" Then, on the second day, I said to myself, "Well, wait a second, Annie. There's a lot of plumbing and rewiring that's taken place, so it's going to be normal that you may have these feelings. Don't let it become a problem. Don't think about it. These feelings are going to go away." It happened about three or four times the first day, no more than two times the second day, and that was it. Later on, as I became more familiar with my new genitalia, I realized that what I'd actually been feeling was not so much the phantom penis itself but the muscle in that area that is now behind the clitoris. I can move around my clitoris now, and that feels very similar to how I used to feel when I had a penis.

Besides the obvious physical changes, there is one big thing that the surgery changed, and although it is something that I cannot explain, and didn't expect, I'm thankful for it. Every day of my life, especially since I was about ten years old, I thought about being a woman. I would watch a woman, just the way she moved or the way she was dressed, and would think about being her. I had also spent so many hours looking at women in airports when I was traveling for work as Ken. There was always that feeling of wanting to be a woman; it never went away! But after the surgery, it was gone. I don't totally understand why this feeling disappeared, because there is no type of neuropathway going from the surgical site to the brain. But the human body and the brain are amazing. After having the procedure, not once have I thought about being or becoming a woman. I just *am* a woman now. And it's amazing to me that my brain recognizes this as a fact. I haven't talked with other people about this issue specifically, but I assume that other post-op patients have had the same type of experience. I hope so. I will address regrets later on in the book, but I had no real regrets about my physical changes immediately post-op. There was no crying, as I wasn't particularly emotional. There was not any dramatic transformation or revelation. My recovery was stressful but undramatic. Without question, the most emotional aspect to me was dealing with my wife, not the surgery itself.

In terms of the physiological aspect, I didn't have a lot of pain at the surgical site. The greatest discomfort I experienced was the extreme soreness of my lower back from not being able to move those first few days. One thing that I was glad about was that I had made the decision not to have a breast augmentation done at the same time. Surgeons are eager to promote this; they make the case that since you're having anesthesia, they should do everything at the same time. I have been a provider for forty years; I understand what the deal is. Having two surgeries at the same time makes for a bigger-priced procedure, and it is a more economic use of the surgeon's time. That said, it can be very convenient for many patients. Maybe the extra money for anesthesia is an issue for some people, or maybe they have limited time away from work. I was not fixated on having breasts right then, and I realized that if I were healing from a breast augmentation at the same time as

I was healing from the genital surgery, it might make me uncomfortable. So, I chose not to have the simultaneous augmentation, and I still believe that that was a good decision for me.

LONGER-TERM ISSUES

Over the next six months, the most significant issue I was dealing with at the surgical site was granulation tissue. I had lost a little bit of the skin graft on part of my labia down near the vaginal opening. The labia come down to a point on each side, and one very small section of the proximal end of one of the grafts just never took, for whatever reason. Sometimes a skin graft will slough off if the blood circulation there has been compromised. This bothered me right from the beginning, and I later addressed it with my surgeon. I had also discovered that if I was standing up and I placed a mirror between my legs, I could see all the way up into my vagina. My labia did not come together all the way down. I was not comfortable with the way this looked, and I eventually asked my surgeon if she could make the labia a little closer together. She said, "If I make them closer together, it will make it difficult if you want to have sex with a guy. That's just the way it is."

The healing process takes all kinds of turns. At one point, while home in Old Field, I was checking on my vagina and was concerned that I seemed to be losing more of my labial skin graft. When I called the surgeon's office, the receptionist told me to send a picture. So, I took a picture with my phone and sent it. When I was about to send the picture, I thought, "I better send this to the correct phone number, because I don't want to accidently send it to a friend. How awkward would that be? 'Here's a picture of me with my brand-new vagina that looks like it's pretty beat up, but don't worry, it's in the process of healing.'" Fairly quickly, I received a response about what I should do about the skin graft. The truth was, I couldn't do much about it, but the doctor reassured me that there should be no further loss of tissue.

However, the biggest issue for me, and I think many patients share this, was the amount of granulation tissue. Granulation tissue is this ropy, mucus-like stuff that oozes from the skin grafts, and it never ends. You try using gauze pads and you try pulling it off, and you try debriding the skin grafts to get rid of it. But as you're healing, and as you're dilating, there is a lot of this granulation tissue to deal with. In fact, even six months after the surgery, I still had some granulation tissue challenges. I had to keep going back to the surgeon's office so they could treat it. The granulation tissue on the back wall of the vagina had to be addressed, and this is something that cannot be done predictably by oneself. This is important, as the granulation tissue is part of the overall healing process, but the excess tissue needs to be removed. The surgeon's team would hit the granulation tissue with silver nitrate, which acts as a cauterizing agent and assists in the debridement of tissue. I didn't mind going back for the recalls, and I followed doctor's orders every time. Additionally, I found that I liked going back. I enjoyed speaking with the entire staff very much.

My surgeon's physician assistant was amazing. The PAs and the nurse practitioners are the people you spend most of the time with in any doctor's office. They become your confidants. They become your shoulder to cry on, and they do a lot of the work in the treatment rooms as well. They measured the length of my neovagina, compiled the evaluation, and got everything prepared for the surgeon. When she finally came in, everything was set up so as not to waste time. I was very thankful for how thorough they were. In my case, these repeat visits went on for months. I remember at one point when I was doing pretty well, maybe seven months after the surgery, I asked my surgeon, "How long is it before I don't wake up every morning wondering whether I made the world's biggest mistake?"

In a nanosecond, she told me, "Four to five years!" I was stunned. No one had mentioned anything close to that before. I had been under the impression that I would be completely comfortable in my new body in maybe two and a half years. Well, as it turns out, that estimate of four to five years is absolutely correct. This is something to consider if you are contemplating a complete physical change of gender at a mature age. You're going to need that extremely long time span to heal and mentally adjust.

BREAST AUGMENTATION CONSULTATION

Eventually, I was healed enough from my "bottom surgery" that I wanted to have a consultation about doing a breast augmentation. Most gender surgeons do both bottom and top surgery, so I was able to have a consultation with the same surgeon who had performed my vaginoplasty about my breasts. I told the surgeon and her PA, "I want the smallest size possible." They both just looked at me, so I said, "Let me repeat that: I want the smallest size possible." I explained, "I'm very athletic. I have worked as a model. I've seen a lot of models with small breasts, and I don't want to have huge breasts." In my opinion, many transgender women choose breasts that are too large for their frames, and that choice makes them look unrealistic. My goal was to look like a real woman, and hopefully, a classy, sophisticated woman. My dream was to pass at a University of Pennsylvania alumni dinner. So I said to them again, "I would like the smallest size possible." The surgeon listened, vacillated over a couple of different sizes, and finally selected a size that was appropriate. We decided on a 300 cc classic profile silicone implant that I liked. In fact, I had done a lot of reading on the topic of breast implants, and I knew a lot of people who had silicone implants, especially some of the transsexuals I knew in Japan, so I was very comfortable having silicone implants, rather than saline. The next decision we had to make was whether to go under the muscle or on top of the muscle. Most breast implants these days are placed under the muscle for better aesthetics, but due to my lack of breast tissue and the fact that I was very athletically active, we made the decision to go on top of the muscle. That was totally fine with me. I just wanted something that would allow me to look good in a bathing suit or a deeply cut dress, and I wanted to be able to buy clothing off the rack. Generally, a trans woman's rib cage and shoulders are much bigger than that of natal women. I'm at the top end of that natal woman limit. So if I had really large breasts, I would never be able to buy anything off the rack. I was comfortable with the size we selected and decided to have the augmentation procedure in June 2014.

BREAST AUGMENTATION SURGERY

I arrived at my surgeon's office the day before my top surgery for a final pre-op consultation. This was to confirm all the details that we had discussed months before. I expected to have the consultation with my surgeon, but she was not there. So, I had the final pre-op consult with the physician's assistant instead, and she reviewed everything we'd discussed. She also mentioned that the doctor was going to do a "little lift" of my breast tissue in conjunction with the augmentation procedure. I was surprised but considered that very thoughtful. I was pleased.

This time I had a dentist friend with me as my escort, and the next morning we went over to the hospital. The preparation for this surgery was similar to that of the genital surgery, and I already had an IV line attached with a sedative when my surgeon came by to check in. She asked if I had visited any local restaurants, and after I answered her, I added that the PA had mentioned that she was going to do a "little lift" in conjunction with the augmentation procedure, and that I was most appreciative. This seemed to really irritate the surgeon, and she responded by pushing the surgery schedule directly in front of my face and repeatedly pointing at her scheduled operating room time, which listed only a breast augmentation. Angrily, she said, "See this? This is what I am doing, only this. The other thing is a different procedure. All I'm doing is what's on the schedule." I couldn't believe she was so angry, since I was just confirming what her PA had told me. I was totally stunned, but before I could respond appropriately, the sedative took effect, and I passed out.

After I was released from the hospital, I went back to my hotel room with Walter, my dentist friend. I was scheduled to return to the surgeon's on Monday for a post-up visit, so I had a chance over the weekend to view my implants. There seemed to be something off about them. I know that it can take time for implants to come down the chest wall, but these were not even in line with each other! I was so angry, not just about their poor placement but about the way I had been treated before surgery.

When I returned for the post-op visit on Monday, the PA greeted me just inside the door and offered a vague apology for telling me that I would be getting a procedure the surgeon never intended to perform. I actually felt bad for the PA but appreciated her apology. After my surgeon inspected my new breasts, she decided that I should wait six months and then we'd reevaluate them. This appeased me somewhat, and I generously thought, "Well, anyone can have a bad day."

I returned in December, and at that visit, my surgeon performed a minor in-office procedure that improved the appearance of my left breast, which was significantly lower than the right one. My breasts were still quite far apart and not ideal, but I didn't want to undergo another augmentation procedure. My surgeon said, "You know, it's not so easy doing this on a sixty-five-year-old."

LIFE AFTER GENDER REASSIGNMENT SURGERY

For fifteen months following my genital surgery, I lived in an androgynous state, hoping to somehow save my marriage and salvage something from my business. I failed miserably on both counts. My brother's response to me of, "I am supportive because I don't want to see you go to hell" was actually refreshing.

Living in an androgynous way throughout 2013 meant going to a restaurant with my wife and having the waiter or waitress say, "Hi, ladies, what would you like?" My wife steadfastly refused to acknowledge the fact that I had become a woman. I had to sneak around and purposely avoid neighbors so as not to embarrass her. It was such a colossal mistake on my part that I thought that I could somehow pull this off. My attempt resulted in a complete waste of a whole year. The only good thing was that it gave me the chance to heal properly from my gender reassignment surgery.

In June 2014, three significant events occurred: the finalization of my divorce, my breast augmentation procedure, and my purchase of a house on Cape Cod. When I left Florida to move into my Cape Cod home following my breast augmentation, I made the decision that from that point forward, I would forever be Anne Koch. I would lead my life completely as a woman.

FOLLOW-UP TO SURGERY

I continued to live with the original surgical results for the next three years, but as time went by, I became increasingly dissatisfied with the way everything looked. I wanted to have my labia closer together. This really bothered me, and my original surgeon refused to listen to my objections. Consequently, I decided to have a consultation with Dr. Toby Meltzer.

Dr. Meltzer is a plastic and reconstructive surgeon practicing in Scottsdale, Arizona, who specializes in gender reassignment surgery. Not only is he famous for having the most experience in the field, but he is considered by many people worldwide to be a great surgeon, especially for male-to-female procedures. Furthermore, he principally performs a two-stage procedure, which means he has the patient back for a second operation in which he fine-tunes the genital aesthetics. (I will discuss the differences between a one-stage and a two-stage procedure in chapter 5.) I arranged a consultation with Dr. Meltzer in Scottsdale in May 2017. I was lecturing in Scottsdale at the time, and even though Dr. Meltzer is booked almost a year in advance for consultations, his staff made a special effort to fit me in for a consultation when I was in town. I had met Dr. Meltzer a few times at conferences, but I had never spoken at length with him. I arrived for my consultation and ended up spending two hours at his office. He was incredible during the consultation, and he demonstrated to me that by pulling things in different directions and by doing a little "nip and tuck," he could get a much better result. I also had him evaluate my breast augmentation, and his recommendation was to perform a second augmentation and to put the implants under the muscle rather than on top. I made an appointment for a labiaplasty and revision for November 2017. I decided to wait on the breast augmentation until the second half of 2018.

My entire experience with Dr. Meltzer, including the revised surgical result, was amazing. I finally have what I envisioned when I began this entire process five years ago. I was also impressed that after the procedure, Dr. Meltzer's office would call once a week to check in with me. I finally had to tell them that this was not necessary, as everything was fine. This commitment to follow-up is noteworthy, and Dr. Meltzer himself spent seventy-five minutes after the surgery discussing the procedure and transgender surgery in general with Akiko, who had again acted as my escort, and myself. This was indeed a huge change from my first experience with gender reassignment surgery.

There is another thing that needs mention here. It has now been approximately five years since I had the initial gender surgery. I keep going back to what my original surgeon said to me about the healing process taking four to five years. That statement is among the most honest, no bullshit things I have heard in experiencing this entire transgender journey. It does take four to five years to come to terms with everything, both physically and mentally, especially if you're older. The good news is that I am finally starting to live the life that I always hoped to live—that of a professional woman. I am beginning to really enjoy my life and have become very comfortable with myself.

What I didn't anticipate was my response following Dr. Meltzer's surgery. I have always been comfortable in my skin as a woman and was pleased by my initial surgical outcome, but this new surgical result has energized me in ways that I did not expect. I feel much more complete as a woman, and I am thrilled!

GOING FORWARD

In the next part of the book, I am going to shift the focus a bit and talk in more general terms about surgical options, and I will offer tips that someone might want to keep in mind when thinking about transitioning. Please keep in mind that these tips and opinions are strictly my own, based on my own experiences. They are not a formal prescription.

5 · MY OBSERVATIONS ON THE GENDER REASSIGNMENT SURGERY PROCESS

AT A GAY & LESBIAN Medical Association (GLMA) meeting, I met a physician who had transitioned. This individual had spent approximately $33,000 with one of the genital surgeons, and later attempted to get a phone call returned by her surgeon, to no avail. The doctor told me, "You know, if I paid $33,000 cash in the straight world, I would be getting a Christmas card every week for a year. In the trans medical world, I can't even get a f*cking phone call returned!" I have since heard other such stories. Personally, I have enormous respect for all the surgeons working in the transgender medical field. I believe that everyone who went into this field did so with good intentions. I also think that all the surgeons who practice transgender surgery are brave individuals. I have been in two surgeon's offices when the police had to be called due to unruly patients. Think about that. Over the course of my endodontic career, I saw thirty thousand or more patients, and I never had to call security. Only once, in the residency program that I was running at Harvard, did we have to call Campus Police to remove an unruly patient, but never in private practice. So, these surgeons are well intentioned, well qualified, and brave. However, I also think that these surgeons never could have imagined the dramatic increase in the number of patients coming into their practices, along with the corresponding increase in their annual earnings. How this dramatic increase in income affects the various surgeons and their behavior toward their patients can only be determined on a case-by-case scenario. There are other aspects of transgender surgery that I would like to address in a more general way, and the first of these is the issue of breast augmentation.

BREAST AUGMENTATION

If you are going to have an augmentation procedure as a transgender woman, you must first choose a surgeon. My recommendation is to choose a surgeon who has experience working with transgender women. Most of the trans genital surgeons also do breast augmentations, so this may be an easy decision. Whatever you do, keep in mind that breast augmentation in a transgender woman is significantly different from breast augmentation in a genetic woman because of the difference of a male's physical carriage and body structure as compared to that of a cisgender woman. Men generally have a much larger chest, which extends into the shoulder area. As for the back, men are considerably larger; therefore, many mature trans women are often quite large in the upper part of their chest. All of this affects the breast augmentation procedure.

If you are an older transgender patient, another thing to remember is that if you began hormone administration at an advanced age, there won't be a lot of breast development from the estrogen. The consensus among health-care providers has always been that younger transfeminine individuals taking estrogen will end up with breast development that is one cup size smaller than their mother's breast size. But for the older transfeminine person, this long-standing axiom is not going to apply. Instead, there will be minimal breast development, and quite often the natural breasts, stimulated by the hormones, will be tubular in appearance. Therefore, this lack of "natural" breast development is going to make the augmentation procedure almost obligatory for those transitioning in later life if they want stereotypically nice-looking breasts.

After choosing your surgeon, you need to decide whether your implants are going to be silicone or saline. There are surgeons who place both and who won't advocate choosing one over the other, so the choice is really with you, the patient. I am very comfortable with my choice of silicone implants, and the people I have known over the past few years who have transitioned have chosen silicone as well. Although anecdotal, from what I've learned, there is minimal risk of the implants rupturing. There is a consensus among health-care providers working in transgender health that saline implants create breasts that are not as hard and that have more of a natural feel. But with saline implants, there is more of a concern if something goes wrong. Although not very common, saline implants can leak.

In addition to choosing the type of implant, you also should consider what you want your breast profile to be. The "profile" of a breast implant refers to how wide it is at its base and how much it projects off the chest wall. There are many different profiles to choose from. For example, an implant with a low, or classic, profile is broader at its base and projects less off the chest wall than does an implant with a high profile. Your surgeon will go over all the characteristics of the different implants and profiles during your consultation. Then you can make an informed decision about what you want. (For further information on breast implants, please go to plasticsur-gery.org.) I chose a classic profile and, as I mentioned before, requested the smallest size possible. Even with natal women, there is enormous variation in breast implant size, and the implants don't always look appropriate for their body types. Sometimes you see petite women who have implants that are very large for their frame. While the size of your implants is a personal decision, your choice helps create a perception to the general public of what type of woman you are. Since I am tall and athletic and want to look some-what sophisticated, I don't need or want large breasts. They would just get in the way and wouldn't contribute to the overall impression I would like to make as a woman. One of my girlfriends described me as having an Upper East Side look, which tends to be very preppy and polished. Whether I actually achieved it or not, that's the look I was going for—that of a cool, sophisticated blonde. So, for me, going for the smallest size breast implants made sense. Transgender women often make the mistake of getting breast implants that are much larger than what they actually need. Many times, these implants are being placed on people who have very large frames already, which makes for a top-heavy profile. As a mature woman, do you really want to have all that weight above your waist? It is not that comfort-able to carry around large breasts, which is why many natal women undergo breast reduction. You also need to consider how having large breasts will affect your activities. For example, if you play golf, how would large breasts affect your golf swing? How would they affect your jogging, your tennis backhand, or even your favorite sleeping position, especially if you sleep on your stomach?

Another issue affected by your choice of breast size—which is critical to me but should be important to everyone—is fashion. I like to be able to buy women's clothing off the rack. If you have a man's frame and you're trying to buy women's clothes, it is not easy to find things that hang correctly. Having large breast implants on top of that makes it even harder to find clothing that fits and looks attractive. At that point, you will be stuck wearing formless, loose-fitting clothes. In my opinion, part of being a woman is getting enjoyment out of looking nice and wearing clothes that fit right and make you look attractive. But at the end of the day, breast selection is your choice. Surgeons will put in basically whatever size you want. So, if you go into their office looking like an offensive tackle for the New York Giants and you want extremely large implants, they will give them to you.

Another aspect of breast augmentation that merits discussion is the nipple-areola complex. Natal women's nipple-areola complexes are not only bigger than those on their male counterparts but also lower on the chest. When you have a breast augmentation procedure as a transwoman, the surgeon generally doesn't do any manipulation with the nipple-areola complex you already have, so the augmented breast may end up looking a little unnatural. In the future, I think we will see surgeons make more of an effort to place the nipple-areola complex in a more feminine position; in the meantime, you should be aware of the size of your nipple-areola complex relative to the overall size of your breasts. For transwomen with small nipples and small areolas, one thing that can be used to make their areolas look more proportionate and improve their aesthetics (other than tattoos and increased growth stimulated through nipple rings) is progesterone.

Progesterone can be taken orally in pill form or used as a cream. Being an older individual, transitioning in my mid-sixties, I was concerned about the blood clotting and sodium retention that sometimes happens when one takes progesterone. Also, people who take a lot of progesterone tend to get really bloated. Therefore, I prefer using a compounded progesterone cream prescribed by my doctor, which I rub into my nipple-areola complex. The cream gives me a larger and deeper colored areola, the look of which I like, and it has also increased the size of my nipples. Has it made my nipples as large as those of an aroused woman in *Playboy* or *Penthouse*? Absolutely not;

not even close. But it gives me enough of a profile that if I'm not wearing a bra, you can certainly see two feminine nipples, and that makes me very happy. But again, the key to developing this growth is remembering that it comes from the progesterone, not the estrogen. Progesterone is not used by many providers in cross-sex hormone therapy, but there are some out there who do use it, so you should feel empowered to ask about it if you are concerned about the size and color of your nipples and areola. Not everyone cares about this to that extent, but an informed patient is a stronger advocate for what they want, and if you're becoming a woman, you should become the woman you really want to be.

In terms of timing, it is up to you if you wish to have your breast augmentation done at the same time as your vaginoplasty surgery or split them into two procedures. From the surgeon's perspective, it makes sense to do both procedures at the same time. The patient is already asleep, and it makes the best use of the doctor's operating room time. Plus, it saves the patient money in terms of hospital stay, anesthesia time, travel time, and time off from work.

Depending on where the implants are placed, the healing period can vary significantly. My augmentation was on top of the muscle, which has very little discomfort associated with it compared to implants placed under the muscle. I took just one Tylenol, simply because I felt I should take something, but I had no pain whatsoever. However, the vast majority of implants these days are placed under the muscle, and that can make you sore. Speak to any of your friends who have had an under-muscle breast augmentation procedure done, either transgender or cisgender women, and see what they say. If you're young, that whole issue of being sore and not being able to move around while lying in bed may not be a big deal. But if you're older, you may want to give yourself a break and perhaps do your surgeries in two stages. I am certain the surgeon will try to discourage you from splitting the surgeries, and again, there are some older transgender women who have done them both at the same time and been fine. Their attitude is that since they are lying there and cannot move anyway, they may as well have the breast implants done at the same time. As I relayed before, one of the reasons I delayed my breast augmentation procedure was that I was foolishly trying to salvage my business, my professional career, and my marriage. When I had my gender reassignment surgery, I was still pretty flat chested, so I figured I could still pass as an androgynous individual. I spent a whole year that way, trying to salvage my old life; in retrospect, that was a wasted year. If I knew how things would shake out, I might have elected to have both procedures done at the same time myself and not wasted so much time.

Your surgeon will go over how to maintain your implants once you are healed, and you'll have several follow-up visits so that the doctors can make sure that everything is going according to plan. When the implants are initially placed, they are very high on the chest wall, but they come down in time—gravity pulls them down, like everything else. And if you are not entirely happy with where your implants are, the location of your new breasts can be manipulated pretty easily. A little bit of tweaking can be done here and there, usually in the doctor's office as a separate no-charge procedure. Once your breasts are positioned where you want them, your next follow-up appointment might not be for another three to six months. The surgeon will then take a look at how the implants are sitting on your chest wall, and you can decide as a team if there is anything that needs to be adjusted.

ONE-STAGE VS. TWO-STAGE VAGINOPLASTY (INCLUDING LABIAPLASTY)

Your genital surgery can be performed in one or two stages. A one-stage vaginoplasty means that everything is done in one shot. The penile inversion technique with dorsal sparing is the technique most commonly employed. Penile inversion basically means that the surgeons disassemble the penis, invert the penile tissue, and reposition the urethra and a greatly reduced glans penis at the appropriate locations. Dorsal sparing means that after the penile skin is rolled down along the shaft, the doctors preserve the nerve that runs along the top of the penis to the glans. Preserving the nerve along the dorsal part of the shaft helps ensure that the neo-clitoris will be sensate. The glans itself is greatly reduced, and this will serve as the neo-clitoris. The labia majora are formed from skin from the scrotum, and the labia minora are composed of inverted penile skin. A combination of scrotal skin sutured to inverted penile skin connect on the inside to form your vaginal canal. A major concern for the surgeon performing this operation is to not push too hard when creating the vaginal vault and accidentally enter the rectum. This complication is known as a rectovaginal fistula and is difficult to repair. If done properly, the final result of a vaginoplasty procedure looks very natural and is both functional and sensate. While the neo-vagina itself is not self-lubricating, there is a lubrication aspect associated with the new genitalia. Both function and aesthetics are attended to during a one-stage procedure, as the surgical team wants to make sure your parts both work and look natural.

A two-stage vaginoplasty procedure was popular for a number of years both here in the States and abroad. During the first procedure, the surgical team would do the conversion surgery to create the neo-vagina and all the other critical anatomy, making certain that everything functioned and looked acceptable. The patient would return three to six months later, and the surgeon would perform the second stage, principally a labiaplasty. Nowadays, some cisgender women choose to have a labiaplasty to rejuvenate the appearance of their genitalia, particularly if they have had a few kids and want to "tighten things up." For a transwoman experiencing a two-stage procedure, the second visit would entail the surgeon fine-tuning the aesthetics of your genitalia. This involves hooding the clitoris and thinning out the labia, if needed. These days, one-stage surgery is promoted as accomplishing both steps at the same time.

I hadn't really thought about the difference between one-stage and two-stage surgeries until after having had my own genital surgery five years ago. I now realize that I have a direct analogy in my own professional world. I am an endodontist. For many years, endodontists did root canals in two visits. Especially when a patient had necrotic teeth, we would medicate the teeth between visits with different types of antibacterial agents to kill the bacteria. A number of years ago, endodontists started doing root canals in one visit, or what we called single-visit endodontics. The success rate was similar to that of performing the procedure over several visits, but there was a huge difference, which I imagine is also the case for plastic surgeons choosing between one- and two-stage surgeries: it was far more profitable for the endodontist to do a one-visit procedure than to stretch it over two visits. If the doctor is doing an $1,800 molar root canal and can do it in sixty minutes, that makes more money than stretching it out. Each part of a multi-visit procedure is going to take forty-five minutes to an hour, which boils down to earning $1,800 over two visits instead of doing two sixty-minute molar procedures in that same time frame (and earning $3,600). Single-visit endodontic procedures are also very convenient for patients: they don't have to come back for another visit, take extra time off, or get numb multiple times. At the end of the day, though, the greatest beneficiary of single-visit endodontics is the endodontist. I have performed over twenty thousand root canals, and about 60 percent of them were done in a single visit. There were, of course, certain cases that I felt I wanted to do in two visits due to the specific nature of the case.

The same kind of thing exists with genital surgery. I think the reason that single-stage surgery is so popular now is that many patients don't have an overwhelming desire to fine-tune the aesthetics of the genitalia. They are just thrilled to have had their procedure done at all—and to have survived it. Most of the time, a one-stage procedure is enough—everything works and looks acceptable. But sometimes it does make a difference. One of the most famous surgeons in this specialty, Dr. Meltzer in Scottsdale, Arizona, still employs a two-stage technique and enjoys an incredible reputation. He performed a one-stage procedure when he began his career, but he later advanced to a two-stage procedure. Concerning his thoughts on this issue, Dr. Meltzer wrote a column called "Vaginoplasty Procedures, Complications, and Aftercare" that is posted on the website of the Center of Excellence for Transgender Health (transhealth.ucsf.edu). In it, he writes:

A common outcome of penile inversion vaginoplasty performed in a single stage (a "one stage" vaginoplasty), with penile skin positioned between scrotal skin, is labia majora that are spaced too far apart. There may also be minimal if any clitoral hooding (except in heavier patients) and the labia minora may be insufficient after one operation. Although there are different variations of the one-step procedure, it has been the author's experience that these previously mentioned deficiencies are common. This constraint is due to factors inherent to the penile inversion approach and the limitations of the blood supply. From the standing position and with the legs together, most results appear acceptable; however, upon direct examination or intimate view, the deficiencies discussed above will be apparent. In order to adequately address these deficiencies, the author believes that a second operation is required. A secondary labiaplasty provides an opportunity to bring the labia majora closer to the midline in a more anatomically correct location, provide adequate clitoral hooding, and define the labia minora. In addition, there are many variables that can affect healing and the final result. Specifically, this secondary procedure also allows the surgeon to deal with differences in healing, such as revision of the urethra, correction of any vaginal webbing or persistent asymmetries, or revise scars that are unsatisfactory. These revisions will improve functionality and the final outcome for the patient and might not otherwise be addressed.

I completely agree with Dr. Meltzer. Even after four-plus years, I discovered that if I stood erect and placed a mirror in front of me, my labia didn't come together, and you could see all the way up into my vagina. When I mentioned this to my surgeon, along with the fact that the labia were asymmetrical, I was told that was just the way it was and that I should just get over it, which, as you can imagine, was a very unsatisfactory answer. I know female anatomy very well, and most assuredly that is not the way it is!

I think if you are an older individual and you don't have the need to impress a new partner with how great your genitalia looks, perhaps the aesthetics from a one-stage procedure are good enough. However, if you want the most realistic, drop-dead gorgeous genitalia, I think a case can be made for having it done in two stages, regardless of what the surgeon says or which surgeon you use. This is a conversation nobody seems to have, and I wish someone had fully explained it to me before my surgery. Yes, there are benefits for the patient of a one-stage procedure, but the business beneficiary is the surgeon. So, depending on your personal desires, you may want to think about a two-stage procedure. Furthermore, and this is something I recently learned, Boston Medical Center and its Center for Transgender Medicine and Surgery is now performing vaginoplasty as a recommended two-stage procedure. I fully expect more university-based transgender programs to eventually adopt this protocol.

When you are experiencing something as complicated as gender reassignment surgery, it makes sense that there will be a recovery period. Many surgeons do an acceptable job with the surgery, but when you take a penis and make it into a vagina, there are a lot of skin grafts involved, and critical tissue is repositioned. It just seems logical that there will need to be some significant remodeling. There's no question that a one-visit procedure is acceptable, and that it will work as advertised. But I'm not talking about the depth of the vagina here. I'm talking about the hooding of the clitoris and the general shape and thickness of the labia and what they look like. Quite often, as Dr. Meltzer mentioned, a single-stage procedure results in labia that are too thick and that don't come together. If you go to a surgeon who normally does a one-stage procedure, they will tell you that they will do a second-stage labiaplasty later on if you are not pleased with the result. This sounds good up front, but you may discover that the surgeon is not too excited about performing a second-stage procedure. However, if you go to someone who is a two-stage surgeon from the beginning, they are going to tell you all the benefits of waiting three months for you to heal before going back and making any changes necessary to complete the look of your genitalia. I sincerely believe this is something everyone undergoing this procedure, young and old, should be made aware of so that they can understand the different options.

There is also another option becoming increasingly popular, especially with older patients, and this is the zero-depth vaginoplasty, or what some call a "dimple vaginoplasty." In this procedure, the surgeon creates female-appearing genitalia on the outside, but there is no vaginal canal. Consequently, this is an easier surgery for the patient, and there is considerably less maintenance of the new genitalia because there is no need to dilate and maintain a vagina. This procedure has become attractive to those patients who have no interest in penetrative sex and who do not want the bother of having to dilate the rest of their lives. I would also assume that this procedure may be attractive to some gender nonconforming mature individuals. It has been interesting to learn from surgeons that requests for this specific procedure come from patients of *all* ages.

Another recent development in the field of transgender medicine is the awareness of the role that physical therapy can play in the healing and maintenance of the neo-vagina. I was first introduced to this idea by Dr. Sidhbh Gallagher at the University of Indiana, and I have recently learned that the Center for Transgender Medicine and Surgery at Boston Medical Center conducts a daylong continuing education course on this topic. The demonstration and use of Kegel exercises makes so much sense to me as part of the aftercare of a vaginoplasty.

SUPPORT DURING THE SURGICAL PROCESS

In this section, I would like to discuss the type of support one needs during the entire surgical process. This is directed specifically toward the mature individual contemplating gender reassignment surgery.

I think it is extremely important for you as the patient to understand what a sea change your transformation can be for family and friends. You are not the only person undergoing gender confirmation. The procedure itself is not easy, as you can see from my story, and you will need an escort throughout the process. Generally, patients choose someone who is a friend or a family member. This is a very big deal for the person who is in the recovery room with you, supporting you—they are going through their own transformation of sorts. They need to do what is right for you medically, in the moment, but they are also processing the end of their relationship with someone they knew well (you, before the surgery) and the beginning of their relationship with someone they are just meeting (you, reborn).

While going through this process, there will come a time when you will ask yourself, What the hell did I just do? This is especially true for the older patient. After surgery, the most important thing to do is to assess your overall health. How are you doing? I think all of us, by a certain age, become tolerant of discomfort, so the pain itself is easy enough to manage, as long as there are no underlying health issues. But the truth is, there are a lot of things to process, including the procedure that was just done to you and the reaction of your escort. You need to understand that this person is most likely not going to be ecstatic, even if they love you. If you have a support person who offers unbridled enthusiasm and support, consider yourself very fortunate. Many mature transgender patients have to rely on a spouse, an ex-spouse, a sibling, or even one of their children, and the transformation is going to be a huge shock to them, even if they think they were prepared. Gender reassignment surgery is that dislocating. It becomes even more dislocating as you start to recover and go back to your day-to-day activities. I will address that later, but to start, I want everyone to be aware that this is a very significant procedure, and you are going to have to be patient with your support system so that they can get used to things along with you.

Everyone is different in terms of pain. I know a number of people who felt that the breast augmentation procedure was far more painful than the genital procedure. I had very little pain in the genital area after surgery. All my pain was in my lower back from not being able to move. When I did move, the pain was intense because of the way the surgical stent was sutured into my thighs. If you are in pain, give yourself a time limit. For example, tell yourself, "I've got to get through this for 72 hours, and after 72 hours, I am going to be a lot better." That will keep you going. Some people read to pass the time, but it's not easy to read while lying on your back. Listening to music helps, and having someone next to you is comforting. Most of the time, you're going to be either sleeping or going in and out of that nebulous half-awake state. There's not a lot of eating in the post-operative period, but again, it's a case-by-case thing. The experience is different for everyone, and I can only suggest what you might experience based on my own transition and the stories I've heard from friends. For me, it was ice chips for a couple of days. Then I got to eat the bun—and just the top of the bun—from a hamburger. I didn't even eat the burger, but it was so delicious! I was so hungry by that point that it could have been anything. It could have been newspaper, and I would have thought it was delicious.

One of the things I was really surprised about during my transition at age sixty-three was the reaction of some very good friends of mine, whom I had known for forty years. I had thought these longtime friends would be incredibly supportive of my decision. Well, guess what? That was not the case. Most of these "old friends" were not overly supportive. Even though they had known me for many years, they had never seen and consequently couldn't understand this part of my personality. They had no idea that I had ever felt like or wanted to be a woman. In retrospect, I realize that my insecurities had allowed me to hide who I truly was too well. On the outside, I was a very masculine, happy guy to everyone who knew me. For them, my transition came out of the blue, and they all felt as if they had been duped and that I hadn't been honest with them all those years. It was quite devastating to me that people I cared so much about, and who I thought would have my back, just couldn't get their minds around my transition. I hadn't changed on the inside—there was no difference in terms of political affiliation or religious standing. But the change in my gender was just too much for the people closest to me to handle. In fact, the people who initially reacted to my transition and surgery positively were the people I knew as acquaintances, not really my best buddies.

In general, women seem to handle a gender change in someone they know more easily than most men, who somehow feel threatened by it. Straight men seem to feel that if they are supportive of one of their friends or relatives deciding to change gender, then other people may view them as being less masculine. My gay male friends did not have a significant problem accepting me as Annie. In fact, they were very supportive. An interesting development has been that after a lengthy period of time, my straight male friends have come back. It began with one or two of my old friends reaching out to me, and after seeing how that went, my other friends came back. They just didn't want to be the first one. Now, several years on from my transition, nearly all my friends have come back, although my relationship with them is certainly different now. I am glad that I didn't overreact when they initially walked away, and I am glad that I was smart enough not to play the "where were you when I needed you" card. I'm glad to have my friends back. I sympathize with them, because I know that a gender transition is not easy for anyone and that sometimes it takes time for people to get used to this new reality. My story should give hope to anyone thinking of transitioning who is worried about whether their friends and family will accept them. I lived through it, and as long as you give people time and space to get used to things and don't overreact to the hurtful words they may say in the moment out of ignorance or fear, there is a good chance that you will eventually have them back.

FOLLOW-UP AFTER SURGERY

After your surgery, the most important thing is to give yourself time to heal. The second thing is to follow the doctor's orders. Please, please, please! There is nothing more frustrating to any doctor than to write prescriptions or give instructions and have patients not listen to you. As you know, I'm a medical professional. I know how important it is to follow things precisely. So, if the doctor says to dilate five times a day, don't dilate twice and think that's enough. Furthermore, the dilating schedule is critical in the post-op period to promote proper healing of the neo-vagina.

You can expect granulation tissue to be an issue. Almost everyone I know who has gone through the procedure has had a fair amount of granulation tissue. It's totally natural to wonder, "Why is the skin from inside my vagina sloughing off? Is my vagina going to fall off?" No, it's not going to fall off. Unfortunately, some people do have skins grafts that fail, and that is a more significant issue that has to be addressed by the doctor. The vast majority of times that people have issues, it's because of our old buddy, granulation tissue. That is why I would also recommend that when you are looking for a surgeon, make sure to speak to some of their patients about their follow-up protocol and aftercare.

A big issue across the board in transgender medicine is that surgical follow-up is generally poor, with few exceptions. To me, good medical aftercare is very important. In other aspects of health care, certainly in dental medicine, there are six-month, one-year, and two-year follow-ups for surgical procedures. For certain other medical procedures, doctors also try to do follow-ups. But this patient attention just doesn't seem to exist at any significant level in transgender medicine. The surgeons themselves would rather be involved in more lucrative procedures than follow-up appointments. I know all the excuses, for example, "Well, my patients come from all over the world, and I just can't keep in touch with them." Another common one is, "They live too far away for them to easily come back." I consider these explanations to be poor excuses these days because of the Internet, and even if the surgeons don't take care of the follow-up themselves, they could have staff members do it. They could even have volunteers! There are so many well-intentioned people in the community who want to help, and they could be used to maintain contact with some of the patients after surgery to make sure they are doing what they are supposed to do and that they are well both physically and mentally. It is so important to maintain contact with post-op trans patients because they often experience a tremendous sense of abandonment as they begin to heal. They have finally accomplished something as dramatic as a gender reassignment, which they have considered doing for a very long time, yet suddenly they feel as if they have been cast adrift. Without follow-up by the doctor's office, they may not have anyone checking on them at all, especially if there are no friends or family in the picture.

Unfortunately, once that surgery is done, once that aftercare is finished and the check clears, you will most likely be on your own. Sometimes, depending on the practice, it can be very challenging to even get a response from your surgeon. Other times, when reporting a problem, you might be told to see your primary-care provider or a gynecologist. In my opinion, that is not the correct response. First of all, I am certain that few primary-care providers have any idea how to work with transgender patients, especially regarding their postsurgical genitalia. Second, there are many gynecologists who have never seen a surgically constructed vagina. And a surgically constructed vagina is very different in terms of its tissue compared to a natal vagina. Going forward, I want transgender medicine to be incorporated into the medical school curriculum, so that all doctors have at least some exposure to trans patients. That seems to be a challenge at this point, but eventually it may happen. I also hope that follow-up care by surgeons becomes more predictable, especially immediately following surgery. This brings me to a bigger issue: continuity of care.

Continuity of care means that there is one medical professional guiding you through the minefield that is your gender transition. Hopefully, this individual can lead you from one specialist to another. Continuity of care can refer to any field of medicine, as it just means that specialty care is connected in a seamless and effective manner. Dentistry has very good continuity of care. Medicine, in general, has mediocre continuity of care, including the extra challenge of coordinating electronic medical records. But in transgender medicine, continuity of care barely exists. Exceptions to this rule include gender centers, such as the Fenway Institute in Boston, and the medical schools affiliated with certain hospitals that are just beginning to establish comprehensive transgender medicine programs.

Continuity of care must be delivered in a better manner in the non-institutional setting. Both doctors and patients deserve to have a better continuity of care. In terms of the surgical aspect of gender reassignment, I want this procedure to continue to be available to patients who need it. I don't want anyone in organized medicine or in the conservative political climate in this country to block gender reassignment surgery. It is an absolutely necessary procedure.

CONCLUSION

I am a strong advocate for gender reassignment surgery; however, I believe patient selection needs to be improved. My feeling is that there are too many people at both age extremes (under eighteen and over fifty-five) having surgical procedures done when there are other options available. With young patients, recidivism and trendiness are issues that must be addressed honestly, without all the identity politics surrounding what, to me, can be boiled down to a medical issue. With older trans patients, gender surgery can have a devastating effect on their lives, and I think more people need to consider whether going all the way surgically is really worth it. That being said, it can be an incredibly rewarding journey. For some of us, there is no choice. We have to do it. But other people considering transitioning need to think things through before taking the plunge and going under the knife.

In terms of choosing a surgeon for your gender surgery, I cannot tell you who to pick. That choice has to be yours, based on your location, your insurance or personal wealth, and what you are looking for, as all of that varies too wildly for me to make general recommendations for particular surgeons. Every surgeon has skills, yet there are some who do things better than others. There are now clinics around the country associated with university and health centers. There are, however, a few qualifications that I can suggest you keep in mind; for example, you should look for someone with board certification in both general surgery and plastic surgery. You could also look for someone who specializes in urology, microsurgery, or ob-gyn. But I think the ideal surgeon has a combination of a general surgical background and a plastics background.

The past few years have witnessed tremendous changes in transgender surgery, and this is all good news. There are now three transgender surgery fellowships, and Mount Sinai Hospital in New York deserves credit for initiating this trend. There is also more of a multidisciplinary approach being taken with patients, which is most beneficial. Continuing medical education for doctors (including hands-on sessions) is also being supported by the World Professional Association for Transgender Health. However, one aspect of transgender surgery that particularly excites me is the entry of so many natal women into the field. These women bring with them improved communication with patients and their caregivers, better aftercare, and, most notably, exceptional follow-up. Good things are happening!

There are also many plastic surgeons out there doing a nice job with breast augmentation. I would just suggest that if you're going to have an augmentation, you should ask your gender reassignment surgeon whether they can perform the breast augmentation as well. Many of them will do the augmentation procedure. If for some reason you are not having your gender reassignment surgeon do your augmentation procedure, look for a surgeon who has treated transgender women in the past, because they will be more likely to keep in mind the aesthetic qualities we discussed earlier in this chapter.

6 · THE ROLE OF THERAPY

For many people considering a gender transition, managing their personal relationships is far more challenging than the physical transformation itself. More emphasis needs to be placed on the role of therapy in transgender medicine.

In order to shed light on the ways that therapy can help someone transitioning, I had the privilege of interviewing Dr. Maureen Osborne and have transcribed the edited interview rather than try to summarize her advice. Maureen is a licensed clinical psychologist with over twenty-five years of experience specializing in gender identity issues. She is a longtime member of the World Professional Association for Transgender Health (WPATH) and was honored with fellow status by the Philadelphia Society of Clinical Psychologists. A frequent speaker at gender conferences across the country, Dr. Osborne appeared in the MSNBC documentary *A Change of Gender* and in the award-winning and well-received independent documentaries *Trans* and *Just Gender*.

During our correspondence, Maureen described the trans community perfectly:

> I believe that the trans community is vast and varied, with all manner of perspectives represented. The main thing they all share is the struggle to be authentic, to be known, to be heard and received. It is truly a civil rights struggle and in the larger frame, a paradigm change for the way we think about gender.

The following is our interview.

ANNIE: I'm here today with Dr. Maureen Osborne, speaking about the role of therapy and how, more specifically, it relates to the mature transitioner. I think the first question, Maureen, is, How would you define the role of therapy for mature individuals, those fifty-five and older who might be thinking of a gender transition?

MAUREEN: I think that therapy is important for anybody who's seeking to resolve gender dysphoria. But I think for older people, it's critical, because older people have a lot more to lose. They might have a history of a long marriage, maybe two to three marriages; they've got their life's work, their life's investments. [Though] that's not true of everyone of course. Some people who are older are actually at exactly the right place [to transition] because they've taken care of their life obligations. Maybe their kids have grown, and they've achieved what they wanted to achieve in their careers. But the issue is that it's harder to transition when you're older. It's harder to be happy and to have a happy life when you've had so many years under your belt in one gender.

ANNIE: Well, what are you trying to accomplish with therapy in these older individuals? In other words, what would be, or what is, in your mind, the ultimate goal?

MAUREEN: I think the ultimate goal is stated very clearly in the WPATH Standards of Care, and that is defined as "lasting comfort with the gendered self." So, in other words, people come to talk to me about their gender dysphoria. Their assigned gender is a source of extreme [psychological] pain and discomfort to them. The gender that people see them in, the gender that they have to perform in every day, doesn't feel authentic. So, the idea [of therapy] is, what can they do to address that? Most of the time, an older person has been fighting really hard to *not* do anything about it. Occasionally you'll get somebody who has had sort of a plan in their mind all along, and they knew that when they reached this point [in their life] they were going to transition. But most of the time [my patients] are people who never expected to do this and who just ran into a brick wall. We've talked about this in therapy groups that I've done, called Hitting the Wall, where there's nowhere to go, and [the decision to transition] feels like life or death.

ANNIE: How different is the role of therapy in the mature transition of someone sixty to sixty-five years old, and how do you approach that as compared to a younger individual, somebody thirty years old or maybe even twenty years old?

MAUREEN: Well, in some ways I think it's easier [to treat someone older] and in some ways I think it's harder. I think the easier part is that an older transitioner usually has very clear distinctions in their head about what they most want to accomplish. They usually transition to the other gender, and they don't have a lot of ambiguity about it. They've waited a long time, and they've reached the point where they often have had some experience, like a life-threatening situation or the loss of someone important in their lives, that makes them think, "Oh my God, I've only got so much time left." So, they feel ready to make the change. [They] don't really have to wrestle with, "Well, what is it? What gender am I? How do I want people to think of me?" But the harder part, of course, is that they've had sixty or sixty-five years of role training as one gender and they've been essentially acting a part.

ANNIE: There seems to be a bit of an increase in people coming forward at a mature age and expressing an interest in transitioning. That's just my opinion as a layperson. But does a sense of mortality become, in your opinion, an all-consuming issue for the mature transitioner?

MAUREEN: I don't know about "all consuming," but the sense of mortality is always present. [But] I think that sometimes it is present in someone who's twenty years younger [as well]. They feel as if—and in fact, to be honest, I've had people who were seventeen say this also—they feel that they've wasted their whole life. But clearly the reality of being older is such that you, um . . .

ANNIE: I think when I describe a sense of mortality, to me I equate that with the thought that I have to transition before I die.

MAUREEN: Yeah.

ANNIE: So, you know if you're sixty-three, sixty-eight, seventy-two, or whatever age you may be . . .

MAUREEN: Yes. I'm sure that there's a very clear correlation between age and the sense of mortality being part of the equation.

ANNIE: Let's move on a little bit here to families. One of the things I've thought about from my perspective is that I don't know whether people who are considering transitioning realize how nuclear it can be to their lives and how much collateral damage can be generated. I've seen it when I've toured recovery houses that are associated with various gender surgeons that I know, and some of these patients come in, and they are thinking about transitioning, and I see the individual, and they will be a certain way. And the spouse will look like they were hit by a neutron bomb. So, how do you address the issue of family relationships? And is this an especially bad problem for someone who's been with a spouse or a partner for let's say twenty, twenty-five, thirty years?

MAUREEN: Right. Well, let me say that [family situations are] a very individual thing. I think that there are people who come in [to see me] who are much more fearful about the damage that's going to be done than they need to be, and there are people who aren't fearful enough. It depends on how serious their orientation is toward the well-being of people in their family. Sometimes people come in and they are convinced that they will destroy everyone in their family. And, other people are like . . . you know, just steam-rolling through the whole process. So how do you address the family? Well, the first thing that I do is that I find out who the important people are in your life. Who is your family? I ask, do they know about you? Because a lot of times they don't when [the patient] first comes to see me. I start them on a path toward finding a way to raise this issue with their loved ones. They absolutely have to, in my opinion. In fact, I won't go forward with anyone if they're not going to tell their spouse. And I rarely will condone someone, for example, starting hormones if they haven't told their spouse. Because I feel that I would be colluding with some kind of a fundamental dishonesty.

ANNIE: I totally agree with you. I am amazed at how many people have started this without informing a spouse of like thirty years. I think that's incredible.

MAUREEN: Well, you know, Anne, there are a lot of people who are single- minded and selfish about how they pursue their life goals. I wouldn't say that transgender people are more so. I'd say that they are actually less selfish than other people, in my experience.

ANNIE: Well, as someone who has actually transitioned at a late age, I think there's just an enormous, enormous amount of guilt associated with it.

MAUREEN: Absolutely. Absolutely. So, you know, when I bring up the subject of family, and what I usually mean in the case of an older transitioner are spouses and adult children, [although] siblings are probably a part of it, too. But most of the time siblings are less directly affected. There might be aging parents, but that's another, somewhat more peripheral thing. But it's partners and children [that I'm mostly concerned with]. And we need to start talking very early on in therapy about the various ways that the [patient can] address their gender dysphoria and how it might impact their family. Really, you know, I don't just assume that people are going to transition. Although older people who come in [to talk about] this usually have that intent. But I do know that thirty years ago you were told, "If you're going to transition, you need to get a divorce and you need to go somewhere far away." It never made sense to me that you would tell a person to do something that's as hard to do as a gender transition and then take away their support systems, too.

ANNIE: What is your sense of true spousal support?

MAUREEN: That's a loaded question. Do you mean true and total? I've seen it occasionally. But I think . . .

ANNIE: I think it's really rare.

MAUREEN: Oh, sure, because . . .

ANNIE: That's not what they signed up for.

MAUREEN: Because people marry, and marriage is a very gendered situation. Even if it's a same-sex marriage. You marry a person of your own sex or the opposite sex, and that's an integral element of the marriage contract, really, for most people.

ANNIE: Yeah.

MAUREEN: I mean, that may be changing now with younger people, but for most people, you know, so I am a woman and you are a man, or I'm a man and you're a woman or we're both women or we're both men. This is the nature of the contract. So when that contract changes in the most radical way, then maybe I'm not really a woman or maybe I'm not really a man. That shakes everything for a spouse. It isn't quite the same for other people [in a patient's life]. But for a spouse, [gender is] in the nature of [the relationship].

ANNIE: How do you process a transition that you know is clearly going to be nuclear?

MAUREEN: Um, well, I'm going to reframe your question, because I don't know for sure that a transition is going to be nuclear. I might see that there are a lot of potential problems. And I *can* usually see it! So, let's start with the beginning. First, to remind you, I find out about the central people in [a patient's life], and I try to assess the strength of those relationships, the strength of the connections, and then I always ask them to bring their partner in. Of course, that's once they explain [their desire to transition] to them or raise the issue with their spouse. I ask them to come in, and I try to get a feel for the spouse's ability to kind of take this in and roll with it a little. I mean I don't ever assume that a spouse *should* roll with it. I think the spouse has every right to say "This isn't for me." I think that my bias is in favor of the long-term, invested relationship. Because I know they can be preserved; I will certainly try to assess whether or not this is something that can be worked out.

ANNIE: That goes right to my next question, which is, Do you try to find or suggest alternate pathways or options for a patient instead of a surgical transition?

MAUREEN: Well, of course I do. I mean, you know, surgery is the final step of a long process in which someone is, at each step of the way, trying to decide if *this* [step] is adequate for them to feel comfortable in their gendered self, right? Finding that lasting comfort with the gendered self. So, it might be that there's a way to have some relief and start really light. Let's say they go out once a month as their preferred gender or as their desired gender, however you what to think about it. And the partner can say, "Okay, I think I can live with that." Some partners can't live with [even] that [much]. And some partners don't want anything remotely having to do with that other gender in their home, and they will say, "You need to get an apartment or someplace [else to be your other gender]," or something like that.

ANNIE: Do you think the greater acceptance of that type of intermediate step would minimize or reduce someone's need to have a surgical transition?

MAUREEN: Well, I think it's always a possibility. I think again that depends on the person, but certainly if that person were able to [start presenting as their preferred gender] comfortably, and enjoyed it, and it felt like enough, it would be a great solution. I often joke with a new client, "I hope you're just a cross-dresser."

ANNIE: What has been the oldest age of a patient that you've treated where they fully transition all the way?

MAUREEN: You mean having surgery?

ANNIE: Yes.

MAUREEN: Um, I'm trying to think. I'm going to say seventy, maybe. I mean, I do have people who are in their eighties that I continue to talk to after their transition. Because again, it's a lot harder [when you're older], and they need more support. So, [my advice is] that if you feel as if you left your spouse behind and want to come back to them, I think what you want to do is, as I said before, you want to [transition] in increments. As a therapist, even if the person comes in and says they want to have the surgery, I want to see how comfortable [they] are talking to [their] spouse about this. They might say, "Not really. I don't know if I can do that." I'm thinking, well, you're not going to be able to transition [and keep your relationships intact] if you can't talk to your spouse about this. So I will try to get them to start embodying the person they want to be in some way. It might be [only] in their bedroom. It might be—you know, going out is always a step—going out in an environment that is not especially geared toward trans people, like to a restaurant or something like that, and to see how that feels. And some people will do this and then they'll come home and they'll say, "Ah. Well, that's good, but I'm fine with going back, I'm ready to be Joe Blow again." But for other people, I might ask them, "How did it feel when you took off your girl clothes?" And you know, they'd say, "It was horrible. I felt like I was losing something really important." For those people, it's harder for them to do the part-time thing.

ANNIE: This is a more general question. What do you think is the percentage of people over fifty-five who transition who are female to male versus male to female?

MAUREEN: You know, I wish I knew. [In my] experience, and it's just my experience, I've seen a lot more male to female [trans patients] than female to male. Female-to-male individuals tend to transition at younger ages. I have had a few patients who were in their forties. I've never had anybody start in their fifties or sixties, never. But you know, I'm sure [those people] exist.

ANNIE: What do you do when you have a patient who is intent on transitioning but seemingly has no chance of passing as a member of the opposite gender? How do you console this individual?

MAUREEN: Okay, well this is probably one area where you and I don't see eye to eye. Because I don't think that passing physically and visually [to other people] is as important as passing in [your own mind], as being fully comfortable in not just who you are but your right to be who you are. Because I have seen people who [are] *really* unpassable live very happy and productive lives because they really don't care what people think about how they look.

ANNIE: Are they retired?

MAUREEN: No. They are working. They are working jobs. And they've walked through the world feeling as if they are just as good as anybody else, and they happen to be trans and they don't talk about being trans or whatever. But you know, I frequently tell people, it's up here. [Points to her head] Passing is up here. When you feel that you are, you know, the gender that you are embodying, then you are. And maybe people will notice, maybe they'll look sidelong at you, but you don't look at that. And you can be really happy. You can be honest to God really happy and content in [your life]. If you're someone who has always been image conscious and so on, that's going to be a heavier load for you.

ANNIE: So physical appearance doesn't really play a role in your analysis of an individual?

MAUREEN: It doesn't. I will certainly tell them that [living as a woman] is going to be tougher for them [than a natal woman] because there are certain things that can't be modified by hormones and [that] can't be modified by surgery either, so you have to be able to be okay with that.

ANNIE: Do you talk about their general health?

MAUREEN: Well, general health, that's another story. I mean, I leave that up to the surgeons. I don't consider that a rule-out [for transitioning] in any way. But I think a surgeon certainly might.

ANNIE: So for an older transitioner, fifty-five and up—you know, fifty-five to seventy, seventy-two—what would make a person an excellent candidate for gender confirmation surgery in your opinion? Or, who would make an excellent candidate?

MAUREEN: It's really hard to say. I guess I'd have to say that obviously being in good health is better than not being in good health. Although I've seen people who have had health crises blossom around their gender awareness, and that caused them to make drastic changes in their lifestyle. They became healthier, so to speak. But I would say people who are good candidates are people who are not rigid. They're flexible. They don't hold too strongly to having to have things a certain way. I think that you're probably an exception to this, but more accomplished and successful people have a harder time, at least in terms of the adjustment, because they're accustomed to getting a lot of respect.

ANNIE: I have to interrupt you for a second because I think I *have* had a hard time. Here's one of the biggest issues for me. I simply cannot believe how much more difficult it is trying to get things done as a woman, as opposed to being a really successful old white guy. The more successful or accomplished you are, the bigger the shock is. Because suddenly you go from being an accomplished guy to all of a sudden being put into an entirely different category.

MAUREEN: Yeah.

ANNIE: That takes a lot to process.

MAUREEN: Oh, that could be a whole chapter of this book. Because you know, as much as men may think that they really understand what it's like to be a woman, they don't. They just can't. And so, to then step into this whole new arena where they are not seen as worthy and equal to men [can be a shock]. That is something that I talk a lot about in therapy with people who are transitioning to female. I don't do it as a warning, "This is what you need to know." It's more like, "Here's what a lot of women experience. How do you think that would be for you? What would be your strategy if you were dealing with that?" We talk about safety, too, because, you know, natal women have been taught to be much more vigilant about their own personal safety.

ANNIE: I remember the first time I experienced that. The whole transition was over and I was in Boston one night around 12:30 A.M., and all of a sudden I heard footsteps behind me. As a guy, that's usually a non-issue. But as a woman, it's an entirely different experience.

MAUREEN: Right, right. So you have to have a very different mind-set.

ANNIE: I personally think in some ways the physical transformation is easier because the bar is so much lower. You see a lot of little old ladies who look like little old men. You see a lot of little old men who look like little old ladies. So I think at some point you can pass more easily as an older person than a younger person.

MAUREEN: Absolutely.

ANNIE: But what is so much more difficult when transitioning as a mature individual is maintaining relationships that were built over many, many years. I got everything wrong when it came to my relationships. With an older individual, how do you prevent depression, and how do you address the sense of abandonment they may feel if their friends and family reject them, particularly in accomplished individuals? Even if you're successful (and I'll use my own particular case), you can descend into loneliness and feel like a widow if everyone who was close to you leaves. How do you address that with someone who's mulling over how far to take their transition?

MAUREEN: This is a huge, huge issue, especially for older transitioners who are not going to be able to preserve their relationships, which is often the case. Ideally, I feel like they should be in therapy talking to me—in therapy for another ten years, to be honest with you.

ANNIE: Welcome to the world of women. But transitioning is just the beginning. And I couldn't get a phone call returned from my own personal therapist after I transitioned. I see myself that there is an enormous need for follow-up therapy. So many post-op people that I have spoken with haven't had any follow-up therapy. I think the whole idea of transitioning is an ongoing process because there is so much to process.

MAUREEN: I absolutely think so. And you know, I continue to see a few people who transitioned years ago. They're people who are really struggling with this concept of how to reinvent themselves relationally. So, there's part one and part two. Part one is that if you're trans, your previous relationship history is filled with all kinds of crap because you haven't been yourself. You've been playing a role. So, you haven't really developed a mature relationship self. You know, [that of] a person in relationships. You may have a long-term relationship. But if you've been in that relationship as the wrong gender, then something huge has been missing; some big component has been missing.

ANNIE: How do you distinguish between an acute episode and a chronic situation?

MAUREEN: I have no idea what you are talking about.

ANNIE: Well, what I mean by that is, How do you recognize when someone is a lifelong cross-dresser and is fine with that versus someone who feels like they must urgently have a surgical transition?

MAUREEN: Well, I think it's the same as anything else, you know. I mean, I'm really going to assess what brought them to this particular place where suddenly transition was all they could think about. I mean, there's any number of things. Let's say they spent a week dressing or something like that. And suddenly they realize, this is who I am, this is who I want to be, or maybe there's somebody that they've been with who's been telling them, "Well, you're really transsexual; you're not a cross-dresser." You know, something like that. So I try to determine [what they really want].

ANNIE: How do you distinguish between somebody who is a cross-dresser and somebody who is gender dysphoric?

MAUREEN: Well, the labels are not so useful. And I know I've used the words to distinguish them, but both people are gender dysphoric. I mean, it's just that a person who's a cross-dresser gets relief more easily and doesn't need to permanently embody another gender.

ANNIE: Is that the description of fetish? Is that a fetish by definition?

MAUREEN: Being a cross-dresser?

ANNIE: No, the way you were just describing it, getting temporary "relief."

MAUREEN: No, no, no. Because I don't believe that is cross-dressing. There are some people for whom a little cross-dressing is purely a fetish. And that's not *just* cross-dressing. It's usually all bound up in sexual relief. And very typically those people go through this process where they achieve the sexual release and, once they remove the feminine clothing, [feel] ashamed or guilty. I mean, most of the time they just have a few items, like they like the feel of stockings or something like that. But I don't like to get too much into the sexual vs. nonsexual because I think there's a sexual component of everybody who is trans and that at some point in their life, [dressing as the opposite sex] had a sexual charge to it.

ANNIE: I also think there's a distinction between transsexual and transgender.

MAUREEN: Well, I just think a transsexual is a special case of transgender. Transgender is anyone in whom their gender discomfort is a primary feature of, you know, their makeup.

ANNIE: Is there such a thing as somebody becoming gender dysphoric for the first time at age fifty-five? Or is gender dysphoria, to you, something that someone is aware of when they are five to nine years old?

MAUREEN: I'd say that most people's stories are the [ones where they always knew but never acted on it], but I've definitely met a number of people who didn't run into [gender dysphoria] until they were fifty-five. My very first case . . .

ANNIE: I find that so hard to understand. I mean, how do you differentiate gender dysphoria from something else at that point?

MAUREEN: I think if you're a psychologist, you become aware that people's personality structures are very different. So, for example, this first patient that I'm talking about who came to me at fifty-two saw [an episode of] *The Phil Donohue Show* that had a transsexual on it, and he said, "That's me." He never had that thought in his life before that time. But he was a very simple person. He worked in a factory. He had a couple of kids. He had a wife. And suddenly he thought, "Oh my God." So I think that his personality structure allowed him to keep that thought so deeply buried that he really wasn't aware of it.

ANNIE: Is there ever a time when a therapist should or could say no to someone's desire to transition?

MAUREEN: I don't grant permission to anyone. I will, and occasionally have, refused to write a letter for someone who asked me for a letter recommending them for surgery because they had been clearly unwilling to meet even the minimal conditions of the standards of care. And, you know, some people don't use the standards of care. But I find that they've relaxed those guidelines, and I believe that they are for the benefit of the client. So, occasionally I have had patients who are really kind of demanding and who come in with a very hostile attitude toward me. I don't need that, so I just say, "I don't see it the way you do. And I'd like for you to consider some other ways of looking at this."

ANNIE: Going forward, based on your experience with mature transitioners, what is the game plan? What I mean by a game plan is, Do you give certain options a period of time before you say, "Well, that's not going to work. I guess we're going to have to proceed to the surgery route"? Or is there a point where you get the feeling that one of the other options might work better?

MAUREEN: Well, as a therapist, my job isn't to have a treatment plan [for my patients] in the same way that a medical practitioner would. In that case, you have a disease, and these are the steps you need to take in order to cure it. My role is to work with them and to see certain things that I think are going to be really optimal for them. I ask them, the whole way through, anybody that I work with, about things that I've experienced as obstacles for other people in their position, just to get a sense of whether they [have fully] considered this [transition they want to make] and how they are going to deal with it. But my role has always been more Socratic. You know, I can give people the benefit of my knowledge, my resource base, my experience. But I will not tell them what they need to do.

ANNIE: So, therapy is supportive. Educational and supportive.

MAUREEN: It's not just supportive. There's a supportive element, but I want them to come to their own determination about how this decision is such a fundamental life change of stance.

ANNIE: It's incredibly dislocating.

MAUREEN: I will not lead people down a path. I just think that is really irresponsible.

ANNIE: Which leads me to the perfect next question. After a mature transition, what is the best way to conduct one's life going forward? Through stealth? Through titrated reemergence? Is it play it by ear or a case-by-case thing?

MAUREEN: Well, I'm not a great proponent of stealth. That doesn't mean that I think that you should, you know, get up on the rooftops with a loudspeaker and say, "I'm a transsexual!" But for me, and the way that I view things, stealth is a psychologically unhealthy way to live your life. It makes you go from one closet into another closet. And it causes you to have to be deceptive. But the real thing is that it doesn't really allow you to develop. So, when you're stealth, you're playing a different role.

ANNIE: Well, let me just put in a little bit of sidebar on that topic, too. The majority of my life I have lived and worked in the straight world. And now I have an enormous network of great, wonderful friends, from tennis and other things. Everyone just knows me as Annie, or as little kids call me, "Dr. Annie." And you know, I don't say "Hi, I'm Annie. I'm a transsexual." I just say "Hi, I'm Annie."

MAUREEN: Right, right.

ANNIE: But one of the things that happens when a transwoman meets new people is that there are times when you feel kind of guilty that you are not telling the full truth. For example, if somebody is talking about menstrual things, I'm not going to say, "I've never had a period in my life." I'll give an answer, but I don't particularly like lying. So I always have a little bit of a guilty feeling, like I'm pulling the wool over some people's eyes. How do you address that with your patients?

MAUREEN: Well, I believe that there is no right or wrong way to transition. But I think it's important to deeply consider both sides. So, for example, the problem with being unable to fully address the question of what your periods were like, let's say, is that you (a) have to lie if you're going to be stealthy but (b) are not able to be fully intimate and genuine in your relationship either.

ANNIE: Right, but I don't consider it stealth; it's just being smart, and it's being polite.

MAUREEN: Right. But I think that there's a lot to be gained from being honest. From actually coming out and not saying, "Oh, I never had a period in my life" but saying, "Oh, well, I mean, you know, periods, I didn't have a period; you realize that, right?" So basically what you're saying is, "You know about me, right?" So you're not coming out and saying "Look at me, I'm a transsexual!" You're just saying, "I assumed that you knew about me." Being just very low key about it. I think that what I have found is that people's relationships are much deeper once others know fully who they are.

ANNIE: That takes me to the question of follow-up therapy, which is the idea of continuing talk therapy after the gender switchover. I think follow-up therapy is as important as diligence with the genital dilation and facial feminization maintenance. I think it's absolutely critical, and what is amazing to me is that I don't think people do follow-up therapy much at all. So just share with me for a second your thoughts on follow-up therapy, and whether you think therapy ever ends.

MAUREEN: Well, therapy definitely ends. My approach is such that sometimes you reach a point [with your patients] where you're not doing more than just kind of shooting the breeze and chatting rather than doing anything deeply therapeutic. And what I usually say then is, "You know, maybe your time could be better spent doing other things. I'm always here. And if you hit a snag in your life you can always get in touch with me." Of course I believe in therapy. The problem is the standards of care; I mean, this is the downside of having standards of care: When the guidelines started, they stated, "You must have X amount of therapy before you can get the green-light letter." So people take that literally. And they say, "Okay, I had my therapy. I got my green light. I'm done." When really, as you know, they are just beginning when it comes to the ways in which therapy could be really useful to them in making their full adjustments to their new life. And the people who do choose to re-engage with me, it's a whole different level of engagement.

ANNIE: Yes.

MAUREEN: And if they return to therapy after they're really, [truly] free from gender dysphoria, we have the opportunity to dig deeper into areas that they haven't addressed previously because gender dysphoria bottles you up. You become a partial person.

ANNIE: So, what do you think is the difference? What is the great differential that allows some of us to totally compartmentalize our gender dysphoria versus those people who are totally dysfunctional? What's the difference between them?

MAUREEN: I don't know. I think it's probably a very complex equation. I think it has to do with something that we haven't learned how to quantify yet, and that is the level of gender dysphoria [a person carries around]. How much friction does it create [in their life]?

ANNIE: Does intellect play a role, too?

MAUREEN: I think that intellect plays a role. But I think it could be either positive or negative. I think sometimes intelligence is a hindrance. And I do think, as I said before, that you can be a very simple person who isn't very deep and still be able to make the change very easily. Because the thought process is, "Oh, okay, now I'm a girl, or now I'm a boy." And there is no deep thinking about it.

ANNIE: I think compartmentalizing is very challenging.

MAUREEN: Well, some people compartmentalize. Again, this is a brain function; it's a very complex function. Patients do it as part of their personality structure— you know, everything is in a little compartment.

ANNIE: Do you have any sense of the suicide rate of mature people who transition gender, let's say five years out or ten years out from their surgery?

MAUREEN: Um, I can't say in any kind of a percentage. [I don't think there is a simple formula for trans] people who attempt and accomplish suicide when they're older. I don't think they're people, for example, who shouldn't have transitioned or something like that. I think they tend to be (a) people who are prone to depression, prone to deep depression, and (b) people who feel, even when they transition, that they are trapped by the world.

ANNIE: I think from my perspective, and I'm a person with a lot of energy, I think there's an enormous adjustment period in terms of how you're perceived suddenly as a woman, as opposed to how you were perceived as a guy. The toughest

thing is re-establishing yourself in your own field, as opposed to totally rein-
venting yourself. Because if a person who is an attorney suddenly becomes an
artist, it's quite different than staying in the field of law after a gender transition. One of the things that I want to accomplish with this book is to let people
know that you can go back and re-establish yourself in your field. It just takes
time and persistence. And I think that's really important.

MAUREEN: But you know, Annie, you don't really see how there's a gap between
the energy level that you have and [that of] most people. It requires a massive
amount of energy to reinvent oneself. And financial resources, but mostly just
energy and imagination and, you know, the drive.

ANNIE: How do you recommend that a therapist work with a surgeon?

MAUREEN: Um, well, I think ideally [therapists should] have at least some degree
of face-to-face interaction [with the major surgeons in the field in their geo-
graphical area], so that when you refer to a surgeon [by name to a patient,] you
know [something about the person] to whom you are referring. That's ideal.
So part of it is that therapists need to go to conferences and need to meet surgeons. I happen to have been in a professional and collegial relationship with
one of the surgeons with whom I work. So that gave me the opportunity to
know that person much better. But I find it incredibly useful to have a real personal relationship with every surgeon to whom [I] refer patients. And you
know, let's face it, there aren't many surgeons who do this work. So I'm generally going to [have to] respond to someone who might say, "I want to go see
this person," and if I'm not familiar with them, I'm going to say, "Hmm, I've
never heard of him. What makes you interested in them?"

ANNIE: I was very impressed when I heard that one of the surgeons you worked
with met with you every month or every two months and actually reviewed
cases with you.

MAUREEN: Oh, yeah. We did that for a long time.

ANNIE: I think that's an incredibly professional, productive way of helping your
patients.

MAUREEN: Well, you know there are also these gender clinics that get together
and go over cases as well. Usually the surgeons aren't involved in these case conferences. But when the surgeon is involved, I've learned so much more—
things that wouldn't have occurred to me because I'm not a surgeon. I'd say,
"Why are you such a stickler about weight?" They'd explain to me exactly what
having a very overweight patient means when you're doing this surgery, and
so forth. I was lucky enough to actually observe an entire surgery beginning to

end. So, I was able to see [for myself]. Again, though, I leave the health elements up to the doctors. I'm really talking about one's ability to transition sexually, not necessarily to have surgery per se when I talk about their size and so on.

ANNIE: How does the changing political climate affect the thinking of a late transitioner?

MAUREEN: I'm quite sure that [the political climate] does [affect older transitioners]. When you transition late in life, it certainly feels like you have a lot more at stake. And when the political climate is a more conservative one, in which transgender people don't appear to be respected, or given their rights, and are not protected or emphasized, then yeah, I think certainly if I were an older transitioner in this political climate, I would be pretty scared.

ANNIE: I think by many parameters I've been able to transition incredibly quickly, doing everything within fourteen months, and I think I've done it pretty successfully. But I cannot believe how difficult coming to terms with everything is. I thought the physical transformation was going to be the most challenging part of the process when, in fact, it turned out to be the least challenging part.

MAUREEN: Right.

ANNIE: The relationship aspect of transitioning is so incredibly challenging to me. I think relationships start with the family but also incorporate professional ties. This is so key, because if you're older, you run this risk of all of a sudden being forced into an earlier retirement than you had expected. So, you need a plan. I'm sure you talk about this with parents of young people, and I'm sure you talk about this at length with your early middle-aged people transitioning. But it is also important for mature transitioners. A mature person needs to make a plan in case their wife wants a divorce, for example. How much is that going to cost? I live in Florida, so when we divorced, that was half of my assets, gone. How is that going to affect my retirement? How am I going to be able to lead a productive life? So, Maureen, how does a person who is very seriously contemplating transitioning work their way through what is on the Internet and in the media to try to get closer to the truth and somehow become able to sort out all the bullshit?

MAUREEN: I think it's my job as a therapist to really bring to bear everything that I know about the difficulties of transitioning to say, Have you considered *this*? Have you considered *that*? What would happen *if*? But I do think that it's very difficult to [plan a successful transition and think of all the contingencies]. And honestly, I think that we're—"we" meaning [those of us] in the professional community—just starting to get an idea of how damn difficult it is for these patients. But when you think about it, we haven't been [helping people transition] for very long. And most of the time, people who have surgery don't go back to therapy afterward.

ANNIE: Right.

MAUREEN: So those of us who are lucky enough to have some postoperative therapeutic contact with people realize, "Holy shit, it's just started, this whole business of helping someone develop a new gender persona."

ANNIE: I think one of the things that helped me was that I had an image of the kind of woman I wanted to be.

MAUREEN: Right.

ANNIE: I think it's really important for people at a late age to have some focus as to what they want to accomplish from their transition.

MAUREEN: Right. Yes. Absolutely. Although, all some people want to do is retire and go fishing. If they have some kind of support system, which is critical, then that's perfectly fine. I think if they don't have a support system, if they don't have a reliable income, if they, you know, have an unrealistic expectation about what they can reasonably expect from the world, then they are going to have a lot more trouble. I'm going to cover all of that with them. But sometimes, you know, Anne, it doesn't matter. They can have everything against them, but they still feel like they've got to transition or they'll just put a bullet in their head.

ANNIE: I never thought about putting a bullet in my head, but I didn't have much support, either. And I think I have a really strong personality. I have intellect, and I have resources, so I realize that I can work my way through the maze. But the process is so difficult that I think someone who might not have support or resources, it could really be a challenge getting through it.

MAUREEN: Well, for someone like you, who had those resources, you could say, "Well, even if I don't get anybody to be with me, I'm confident that I can get through it."

ANNIE: Right. Absolutely.

MAUREEN: Other people, who don't have those emotional or financial resources, might instead say, "I'm going to gather my support system."

ANNIE: The biggest mistake I made was not joining a support group.

MAUREEN: Yeah . . .

ANNIE: I think a support group for people transitioning is so critical, regardless of age. I see younger kids with so much support, especially some of the transgender guys. I think that whatever can be done to surround oneself with some support, it will pay huge dividends.

MAUREEN: Absolutely. And you know, in addition to just giving you emotional support, it's that feedback from peers that helps you develop your new gender persona. So, you can't just do it in a bathroom. You have to do it with other people.

ANNIE: Absolutely. Maureen, I want to thank you very much for spending this time with me.

MAUREEN: Well I'm glad that we got started talking about this, because it's all very important.

ANNIE: I appreciate the time you have given me. That's it. Perfect!

7 · BEGINNING THE TRANSITION PROCESS

Transitioning is very difficult, especially at an older age. As we've discussed, you most likely have a solid family relationship, with a spouse and children. You have people who have been dependent on you for a long time and have always seen you one way. Therefore, one of the first things you should consider is how this change in your life will affect your family and your spouse. Before actually acting on anything, you should inform your spouse and other family members about your intent. This is extremely difficult to do, as you can see from my own story.

The best way to minimize this stress is to see a primary-care provider or at least a therapist and have them be the starting point for this entire process. Another alternative is to go to a local LGBT center or a university gender care center, where there are people who are familiar with transgender issues. This will get you into a network, and these centers have a lot of information for you to think about as you start your journey. The medical network for the primary-care provider will give you access to a physician or nurse practitioner and will be able to suggest an appropriate therapist for you. Eventually, it will also grant access to an endocrinologist. But the key point is that the physical transformation for the older transitioner is actually the easiest part of this entire process. There is a tendency to think, "Oh, the physical transformation is going to be so difficult." Actually, that process can be managed in a way that is straightforward and effective. The most difficult part of transitioning at a mature age is actually getting a handle on your personal relationships, although of course there is also the financial commitment that comes with transitioning.

Once you have connected with a sympathetic primary-care provider or a gender clinic that has a history of working with transgender patients, they will surely conduct a physical examination. This is important, because transitioning at a mature age places both physical and mental demands on you. They will begin with a basic blood panel. They will also run "labs" in order to measure your triglyceride and cholesterol levels, check your testosterone level, and look for other potential issues. In addition, they will try to get you on a path toward better health. Your overall health is important to take seriously before you transition, because if you are overweight or have high blood pressure, these conditions can cause problems down the road, particularly during surgery but also during recovery. You need to be healthy before you transition, and this includes not smoking. Some physicians are very emphatic about the need to stop smoking before transition. And really, you should quit smoking anyway.

The most important aspect of getting into a regulated health-care system, however, will be the introduction to therapy. I wish I had joined a support group myself, because it is so beneficial. I see young people transitioning who have tremendous support networks, through either friends or groups, and it is incredibly helpful for the person to have such affirmation. It is awful that as a mature transitioner, you are often by yourself, with no one to lean on and talk things over with. Obviously, you are not the only person who has ever transitioned, but when you finally decide to do it yourself, you might find it to be incredibly isolating. Besides, it can be terrifying to change so radically at an older age. I strongly suggest that you get into therapy very early in your transition, and hopefully you will have a situation in which you are getting some continuity of care between your primary-care provider and your therapist. They should talk to each other and work together.

As you proceed with your transition, it is very common to get excited and focused on cross-sex hormone therapy. However, it may take a while before the primary-care provider puts you on hormones. Yes, some of the gender clinics are now initiating hormone therapy quite early in the process with informed consent. However, other clinics may be a little more conservative in initiating hormone therapy. Years ago, there was a requirement that someone transitioning had to live in their desired gender for a full year before beginning hormones, and then there was a period where you had to produce a referral letter from a mental health professional before starting hormones. Currently, most clinics and physicians follow the standards of care generated by WPATH (World Professional Association for Transgender Health), which suggest that the initiation of hormone therapy is at the discretion of a trained medical professional. Within the medical community, there is a tendency to give the mature transitioner (anyone over fifty-five years of age) preference in starting hormones due to the perceived maturity level associated with an older patient. Nevertheless, while you are going through the first few months of therapy, there are some things that you need to start thinking about before worrying about the hormones.

ELECTROLYSIS

One of the first things a male-to-female transgender individual must consider is electrolysis. Electrolysis is a way of removing hair by the root through the application of electric current. People use this method to get rid of hair in unwanted places, such as the upper lip and chin, and if your goal is to become a passable woman, you won't want to have any beard scruff. In my opinion, you cannot start electrolysis early enough. In addition to beard removal, electrolysis has a very positive effect on one's skin, since it will become noticeably smoother as a result of the treatment. A woman's skin is quite different from that of a man, in terms of pore size and smoothness, so electrolysis will help quite a bit if one wishes to live full time as a woman. It is a huge hassle, though. First of all, you must let your beard grow for a couple of days beforehand. This is troublesome if you are dressing as a woman. Second, it's expensive, often running $75 to $80 an hour. Furthermore, it takes a long time for the process to work. Many people who transition may require between 120 and 200 total hours of electrolysis. These days, there is also the option of using laser hair removal treatments to eliminate the unwanted hair. However, laser treatments only work well on dark hair and people with dark skin, such as those of Asian descent. If you have blond, gray, or red hair, it will not work. Consequently, you may end up having electrolysis anyway.

You must find an electrologist that you feel comfortable with, because they are going to become like another therapist for you. They are going to see you come in at the beginning of the treatment as a man, especially if you have a beard. Then, as you start to get a little more comfortable and your beard is not as heavy, you may be going to the electrologist in an androgynous way. After eighty hours or more, you may be at the point where you are still going for appointments, but your hair growth is such that you can actually be dressed as a woman. You obviously want to go to an electrologist who has a lot of experience with transgender patients. Almost every electrologist I have seen has some experience in this regard. But just like other providers, some have a lot more experience than others. It is very important to find a good electrologist because they're going to affect the quality of your skin. Your therapist or transgender support group can give you specific recommendations and referrals as to which electrologists have experience with transgender patients. Again, I would strongly recommend that you start electrolysis as soon as possible, while you are waiting to begin hormone therapy.

Ultimately, if you plan on making a surgical transition, you will most likely have to undergo genital electrolysis. Genital electrolysis is incredibly painful and must be done under anesthesia, usually at your surgeon's office. A physician's assistant or nurse practitioner generally delivers the anesthesia. The reason this is important to get done, and why most surgeons offer the service, is that you do not want to have a beautiful new vagina and have hair hanging out of it. Yes, the surgeons have someone doing a follicle scrape during the actual procedure on the scrotal skin, but most surgeons want you to have genital electrolysis beforehand all the same. Please be prepared for that—and don't be embarrassed. These people have seen many patients with the same type of anatomy as yours. The main thing is to get the genital electrolysis done before your bottom surgery, if you're in fact going that route.

DISCUSSION WITH A SPOUSE

The necessity of talking with your spouse about your intention to transition gender is absolutely critical. The incredibly popular television show *Transparent* is the story of a family whose patriarch is transitioning to become a woman. The show details the responses of each of the family members and shows how they all eventually become supportive, making a positive outcome of such a discussion with family seem almost a foregone conclusion. Well, unfortunately, life is not like television, and not every family is as supportive as the Pfeffermans. In fact, in many instances, the family can be strongly *anti*-transition. As a mature individual, you will have to negotiate personal relationships forged over many years, so having a therapist by your side is critical. I did not have a therapist when I began my transition, and that was a mistake that added anguish to an already fraught situation. Additionally, as I've mentioned, I did not belong to a support group, which was another mistake. It is so important for the transitioner to start to create and build support for their choice among their professional and personal connections. This is because the relationship part of a transition is so difficult.

As you'll recall, in an attempt to be honest about who I really was, I wrote a letter to my wife before we got married. In the letter, I mentioned that my desire to be a woman might be a future problem but one that we could try to address together. Even though I wrote this letter, it didn't make things any easier when I finally decided to transition. When you transition, it is not only difficult for you but also incredibly disorienting for your spouse and family.

FINANCIAL PLANNING AND DIVORCE

In addition to trying to navigate the relationships in your life, you must start planning. One of the first things you have to start planning for is costs. How are you going to finance this change? Even if you have insurance, a transition requires a substantial amount of money. You should be prepared for this and have a plan in place. You should also arrange a consultation with an attorney, just in case, because gender transition often results in divorce. Quite often, these are terrible, nasty divorces, and it's better to be prepared than taken by surprise. I could not believe that aspect of my story. I was devastated when I realized that my spouse, whom I loved, could not handle it when she learned of my plans to transition. This incredibly pleasant woman changed dramatically. At the time, I interpreted her change as a reactionary response to the negative feelings expressed by my business associates. These bad feelings culminated in a divorce that was very acrimonious at times. At the end of the day, the divorce had cost me a significant amount of money as well as much of the life that I had loved and worked so hard to build. We had two homes together, including the one on Long Island, which I was forced to sell at a considerable loss. When I left that house, I took a picture of myself crying because it was so devastating. That house was my dream home, and then to have to sell it because of divorce—horrible! I also had to sell the house in Florida, though that sale was a bit delayed because my spouse was still living there. When it sold, it also went at a significant loss. Therefore, when you are thinking about changing gender, don't just think about the physical attributes, although I know that is what we tend to focus on. Rather, the focus should be on navigating your relationships and figuring out how you are going to finance your transition (and its aftermath).

Part of financial planning is understanding that you may not have spousal support. You may end up with a divorce, and if you go into divorce proceedings, what types of assets are you realistically going to be left with? Think about how you are going to navigate Medicare. You must analyze your own personal insurance situation and any retirement savings plans you have. You must realistically calculate your cash resources, too. If these become depleted, is there going to be enough money for you to survive? Many times, savings are not sufficient to live on in retirement, even without the added costs of a surgical transition. Changing gender is such an important decision that making it at a mature age is enormously difficult.

In terms of facial feminization surgery and other procedures, some insurance companies cover them. Harvard Pilgrim Health Care in Massachusetts covers some facial feminization surgery, such as the nose and the chin. It also covers the osseous part of forehead recontouring. But most insurance plans do not cover these procedures, and most surgeons who do this work charge a fairly significant fee. Therefore, in addition to the cost of electrolysis, you have to factor in the cost of facial feminization surgery as well. And there's more. Almost every male-to-female transitioner I know over forty has had some hair plugs put in, generally in the front of the head at the hairline. This is also not cheap, as it will cost you another $8,000–$10,000. When you start to add everything up, it becomes incredibly expensive to transition. Medicare does not pay for all of these extras, though it *will* pay for some things (it's definitely getting better). But for things other than the most obvious surgeries, you will have to pay out of pocket. Speaking of which, if you have the extra cash, you may want to investigate speech pathology, which can help you learn how to speak more like a woman.

AGE

Age itself plays a huge role here. If you make a mistake when you're twenty, thirty, or forty, you can get up off the ground; you can come back from that.

But if you make a mistake at sixty-three or sixty-eight and have lost both your job and your family, it is very difficult, if not impossible, to come back from that. Be very cautious as you plan your way forward.

Having gone through this process myself and having managed to survive, my suggestion to mature individuals contemplating a gender switch is to ask themselves the following questions, thinking hard about the answers: Is there another way that I can live my truth? Is there another way that I can address my current gender situation without having to undergo genital surgery? Gender surgery changes the entire game forever. You can even have facial feminization surgery and still continue to lead your life in such a way that when you need to look like a man, you can, and when you wish to appear as a woman, you can do so in a more convincing manner. Either way, if you have facial feminization surgery, you will look better and younger as a man or a woman. But at that point, you haven't reached the point of no return. When you undergo gender reassignment surgery, you are going nuclear.

REAL-LIFE TEST

As you proceed with your transition and your primary-care provider has decided it is time to initiate cross-sex hormone therapy, there is a standard of care regarding a "real-life test," in which you must live as a woman for at least a year. As I mentioned before, it's not always strictly necessary, and doctors do have some say in whether you can skip this trial period, but knowing that their patients have done the real-life test is very important to surgeons. There are some surgeons who will look the other way if it hasn't been done for a whole year, and then there are other, more scrupulous surgeons who will not. But as part of the standards of care, they are evaluating how the hormones are working, how you're beginning to live, how you're relating and interacting with other people as a woman. They want to make sure that you're sure. For example, coming out to people in your professional life, how is that going to work? Are they going to ridicule you? Are you going to lose your job? Take it from me: as a male at sixty-three, it was not easy going from a respected senior person in a company to a female who is not viewed the same way.

Something else to consider is that many times, someone who may be attractive as a man may not be nearly as attractive as a woman. But if you can pass as a woman and you can act like a woman, your transition is going to be a lot easier for you. The real-life test allows you time to practice your feminine self. If you cannot pass, and if you do not particularly act or sound like a woman, of course you can transition (and should if you've decided that it is the best thing for you), but your life may be more difficult. Distrust and disrespect can come even from loved ones. Loved ones, I discovered, love you as you were: as a man. When they see you as a woman, and the woman is not nearly as credible to them as you were as a guy, their opinion of you changes. I discovered this myself, especially with people who had known me for forty years. I thought these people would be my biggest supporters. They weren't. They felt that somehow they'd been cheated, that I'd never been honest with them about who I was. I am a person who prides myself on honesty. The *only* thing I couldn't share with everybody was my desire to be a woman.

WORKING WITH A THERAPIST

It is so important that you work with a therapist. I know I've said this many times in this book, but that's because it is very important and the most overlooked part of the process. Please sit down with someone qualified and evaluate the many alternatives to gender reassignment surgery appropriate for someone at a more advanced point in their life. Yes, there will be a certain number of individuals for whom the only solution is gender surgery. I get that—I did it myself. But I have seen cases in which having the whole surgery turns out to be devastating, and once you make that choice, you can't go back. If you are thinking, "Well, someone said on TV that there are no regrets." Wait a second! Generally, the people saying "no regrets" are surgeons working in transgender health care, and not only are they trying to drum up business, but they don't have any kind of follow-up with their patients. They are certainly not speaking with patients five or ten years out from the surgery. Renée Richards addressed this issue in her book *No Way Renée: The Second Half of My Notorious Life*, and I have found that she is spot-on in most things she says. She is a smart, educated woman, and she was well known as an ophthalmic surgeon. She also had financial resources, and yet transition was difficult for her, too. I'm all for gender affirmation. I'm also for gender reassignment surgery when indicated. But it is important for everybody to be prepared and to go into their transition fully informed about the possible alternatives.

Therapists will work with you to map out all the possibilities, and they will help you see your way through the minefield that is gender transition. One thing to keep in mind, though, is that therapists tend to be very good at making patients feel comfortable with their transgender identity, but they are not as good at helping someone become comfortable in a new gender. Regardless of one's physical attributes, I think it is helpful to act like a woman. Of course, acting like a woman can mean many things, depending on what type of woman you want to be, but I think practicing and using women you admire as templates for your own mannerisms will go a long way in making your life easier as you transition.

If you have a spouse who supports you in your journey, count yourself fortunate. In the vast majority of cases, the choice to transition is not what the spouse expected from their marriage partner. Sometimes spouses of mature transitioners who hang in there appear to be supportive, or they try very hard to understand and support their spouse's choices. But in most cases, they're not really on board. In some cases, they may have no other choice but to try to see their way through the process. A spouse at that point is likely to be mature as well. She may have been a mother. She has been a wife. She may not have any marketable skills, or she may not have a lot of her own money. What is she going to do? When you are transitioning, it is not just about you. Your choices affect the other people in your life.

There is, however, a distinct possibility that a spouse will come back after a period of time. Most spouses know about, or at least have an inkling of, their partner's gender dysphoria but try to avoid thinking about it. A spouse may believe that they can help their partner "grow out of it." But when they realize that they have failed to alleviate the symptomology, this is when they revert to anger, recriminations, and disappointment. This is totally understandable. However, after some time has elapsed, some spouses realize that they loved their partner for who that person was, not for their gender alone. Obviously, this is a complicated situation, but if you are truly hoping to salvage the situation with your spouse, give it some time, and don't say things or act in ways you might regret later. Give them time to grieve their old relationship and come to terms with the new one. I do know individuals who had their spouse return to the relationship. Truthfully, many of these types of relationships are nonsexual before the change, so after a gender change, there should be potential for reconciliation. This makes sense to me after having fully transitioned myself. Both parties can benefit from getting together again. As we age, the need for companionship becomes a serious issue for the individual who transitioned as well as for their spouse. This is a very different situation from that of a younger person, who transitions gender and still has much of their life left to develop.

SENSE OF MORTALITY

The sense of one's mortality is often profound for an individual who transitions at a mature age. As so often happens, there is an event that acts as a trigger to start us on the path toward finally transitioning. It may be surviving cancer; it may be surviving the death of a spouse. Regardless of the specific trigger, we are overwhelmed by our own mortality and realize that we have to transition before we die: "I cannot die as a physical man; I have to change my gender before I pass on." This is a sentiment that I hear quite often from people who realize that there is no choice for them other than fully transitioning. If you speak to some of the surgeons who see older patients, they will share the same impression, and I do believe that they give older patients preference.

I cannot stress enough the need to plan ahead while you are transitioning. This is serious business, and I know that you want to transition successfully and to do it as quickly as you can—if you're sixty-eight years old starting out, it's hard not to feel that you are on the clock—but it's going to take a minimum of eighteen months to two years to fully transition. Many transitions can take even longer—for example, if you have to save money between stages or have a health problem during transition—even stretching to four years. Two years is a good estimate, though, and this should factor in to your planning: Where are you going to be in two years?

When you are committed to transitioning at a mature age, it is very important to keep up with your primary care and therapy going forward. Throughout your transition, the doctors will be doing blood panels to monitor your hormone levels, both estrogen and testosterone. This monitoring will continue even after your surgical transition. Having a strong relationship with a good primary-care provider, in addition to a good therapist, is vital to your physical and emotional health and something you will benefit from the rest of your life.

HAVING A GOAL

Part of the pre-transition planning process is setting a goal for yourself. Everyone has different goals. My goal was to be seen by my peers as a professional woman in my industry when attending a University of Pennsylvania alumni function. Others may see themselves as being recognized as an artist or a musician, as an engineer or a teacher, and some may simply want to be seen and live as a wife. Everyone is different, but what is important is that you have that proverbial carrot out in front of you. That way, you have an image of yourself in the future that you can work toward. I found that having that image in front of me really helped me during my transition. Along the way, there are so many things that can potentially knock you off your path, especially for the late transitioner. But having a goal and imagining what kind of woman you want to be will help you move forward in the transition process.

I cannot emphasize enough the need to be organized in terms of when and how you discuss this with your spouse and family members. Everyone will have an opinion—your children, your children's spouses, your siblings and their children, and your other extended family—and they will all feel free to share them. Gender transition is not easy at any age, but it is especially challenging for the mature transitioner.

SAFETY AND IDENTITY

With more and more people thinking about gender transition at a mature age, there needs to be some honest talk to prevent surprises or rejection. One honest point that needs to be brought up is the changing nature of the political climate in the United States. I am not discussing any particular political situation—that is not what this book is about. But you need to keep the political climate of the country in mind if you're planning to transition. I know some people who were thinking about transitioning but then suddenly decided not to because of the increasingly conservative attitude in the country. I think that may have been a wise decision, because if you are not prepared, the sudden public rejection by friends and business associates can be devastating. And once you think through the possible outcomes, you may realize that you're not ready to face that abandonment. I also know people in respected positions who thought, "I'm going to send a letter out to everybody at work explaining my plans to transition, and they're going to be incredibly supportive." Really? What if they aren't? Are you prepared for that? It's not that easy to explain your transition to your co-workers, especially your managers. And it won't be easy for them to get comfortable interacting with you in an entirely new gender persona. It can be done, but before you even consider telling anyone, make sure you are familiar with your company's diversity rules and the laws regarding gender transition and acceptance thereof. You can still be fired in numerous states if you come out as transgender.

Even basic things like behavior and your comportment in the ladies' restroom can be a challenge. As I write this, the bathroom issues are bigger than ever. When I was beginning my transition, I used to plan trips around making sure that I could use a bathroom at a safe place. Driving on a thruway or turnpike, I would think, "Can't I just go in and use the ladies' restroom if I have to go?" Well, yes and no. And since staying safe beats out convenience or logic, you make a decision that overrides the potential danger of using an unknown restroom. Something so basically physiological becomes such a big deal that you have to plan your trip around it. This borders on the ridiculous! It's even an issue in schools now, since people are transitioning at a much younger age.

There are so many levels to transitioning. If the person transitioning is young, some people might interpret the decision as the person "finding themselves." No one gives you the benefit of the doubt if you are over fifty-five. There are always people who throw caution to the wind, and it doesn't bother them if people are uncomfortable around them—they are who they are. That's great, but most of us are not that immune to how people perceive us. Realistically, what is it that you want to be after you transition? Do you want to transition and actually be a woman? Do you want to transition and be your own character? Do you want to transition and be your own kind of third gender? These are all valid goals for your transition, but they are going to elicit different responses from the people you live and work with.

One thing that will help you feel better is to always try to be confident when you feel nervous about your public presentation. It takes just a little extra effort to pay more attention to your makeup and clothing in certain situations, and it can make things much easier for you. You should also consider your demeanor: How do you want to act as a woman? It is good to think this through before you start making surgical changes, perhaps during your real-life test. I am more comfortable with the traditional gender-binary world, but there is a lot of room for variation out there. My experience has been that most surgeons are more comfortable with the binary but are totally accepting of anybody in between. And they get all kinds of requests, both surgeons who work above the neck and those who work below the waist. It pays to think about how you want to move through the world as a woman ahead of time and add that to your goal image of yourself.

Without question, transition is going to be the most challenging thing you have ever done in your life, because it will change your whole life. And it most certainly can include gender reassignment surgery, if that's right for you. Today's surgeons are highly skilled, and in the vast majority of cases, the physical transformation can have amazing and profound effects. But the internal component of who you are and how you feel deserves attention, and only you can fill in those blanks. Going through a transition late in life is about having that last quarter or last third of your life be satisfying, productive, and everything you want it to be.

THE CHALLENGES OF HAIR AND VOICE THERAPY

Electrolysis, as I mentioned earlier, can never start early enough. It's painful and expensive and seems never ending, but at the end of the day, you will have nice-looking skin. Regarding laser hair removal, I don't know any mature transitioner for whom the laser really solved things. In my experience, the permanent hair removal method of choice for mature transitioners has been the good old-fashioned zapping method of electrolysis. In terms of chest hair, I haven't needed to have any laser or electrolysis done on my chest. When you are taking estrogen in combination with Spironolactone as a blocker—and especially if you have had bottom surgery—your testosterone level will dramatically decrease, which will significantly reduce your amount of body hair.

If you're transitioning to become a woman, the hair on your head is a big issue as well. Most mature men, unless you are really lucky, have had some hair loss, either at the temples or in the form of male pattern baldness in the back. Either way, you will get some regrowth with hormones, but generally, it won't be enough to make up for the hair loss in the areas that are very sparse. Mature transitioners will probably need some hair plugs, generally in the

front of the head and in the crown area, as well as some type of surgical procedure to bring their hairline down, which I discussed earlier.

Almost every male-to-female trans individual I know over forty years of
age uses hair extensions. Even some of the younger people I know use them
to create fuller hair and add length. Extensions will definitely help with volume as you get older, so become familiar with the different hair extensions
out there and their various qualities. Some are made from human hair, and
others are synthetic. I like the human hair extensions, but you need to educate yourself. If you belong to a support group or a club, this is an opportunity to share different opinions about the options. Some people wear wigs
instead, and that can work very well. Just make sure not to buy a cheap wig—
they look terrible! I know a number of beautiful transsexual women in their
forties who had such hair loss as men that they wore wigs until they could
get the surgical procedures that would give them enough natural hair that
they could then supplement with extensions. This is just another of the myriad challenges to becoming a woman at this point in your life.

Part of this challenge includes voice therapy. Some of the good news here
for mature transitioners is that Medicare will often pay for some voice therapy. If you go to a speech clinic within a hospital or medical center, or a speech
therapy clinic that works with patients after strokes, you'll find they are generally very kind to the late transitioner, and after you take an initial test, they
will record things in a way that will allow you to have Medicare pay for your
sessions with the voice therapist. Voice therapy should be a component of
transitioning that you seriously consider. It is difficult cultivating a feminine
voice, and for those transwomen who have a naturally beautiful voice, I
applaud you. For most people who transition at an older age, it is far more
challenging to sound natural. An acceptable voice is not just about the pitch
and the tone but about how to speak. One of the things I did for myself when
I first started lecturing on the trans circuit was to try out new voice pat-
terns. Since I loved lecturing as a man and had done it many times, I wanted
to continue to lecture as a woman. At my first trans lecture, a transgender
individual and their spouse came up to me and asked, "How did you do that
with your voice?" I was so thrilled, because having a voice that went with my
persona had been a real concern to me. My voice pitch was okay, but I
wanted to make sure that my voice, in terms of intonation and arrangement,
was in the feminine range. To me, the proof lies in a telephone conversation.

When you speak and someone says, "Yes, sir," that is not a good experience. But if you speak and they say, "Yes, ma'am," that can make your day.

IN REVIEW

In this chapter, I introduced you to some of the challenges you'll face when transitioning. You need to consider all of them and focus on the ones that are most important to you. At the end of the day, though, the most important thing that you should consider is whether there are other options that might work for you at this point in your life other than the full gender reassignment surgery. Think of gender reassignment surgery as a last resort. Perhaps a little bit of facial feminization surgery, dressing as a woman, plus participating in some female activities can work for you in addressing your dysphoria. This is something you should discuss with your therapist, since it could be a satisfactory alternative for many people. However, if you see no option other than fully transitioning, and you feel your mortality weighing on you, you may decide to take the surgical route. If you are going to do it, I want you to plan thoroughly. The key thing about transitioning is to remember that the process is not an end game; it is actually the beginning of the rest of your life. This is so important, I'm going to repeat it: Transitioning is not the end game; *transitioning is only the beginning*. It is the beginning of the rest of your life. It's very exciting, but it's also very demanding. So please, go into this prepared. It is okay to be excited, but don't believe everything you read in the newspapers and the magazines. For sure, don't believe everything you read or see on the Internet. There is some useful information, but there is also a whole bunch of misinformation. Try to surround yourself with people who love and support you, as well as people who are professionals. If you do that, it will help ensure a successful transition.

8 · FURTHER IMPRESSIONS FROM MY TRANSITION

IN THIS CHAPTER, I address my experience with gender transition and the impressions it made along the way in the hope of facilitating someone's transition or even making someone think before physically transitioning at such a late point in life if they don't really need to. I will also address, from *my* perspective, the kind of woman I have become after my transition.

AGING

This book is oriented toward the over-fifty-five transitioner, as there are some very specific issues that come along with aging. As we age, we begin to feel the pressure of our ever-shortening window of time on earth and need to have things done quickly, thoroughly, and properly. Because of the compressed time frame, there is significantly less margin for error for everything in your life, because you feel that you don't have as much time to figure things out "later." Consequently, if you get a diagnosis of gender dysphoria, you must be certain that you are truly gender dysphoric before attempting a surgical solution. Could there be another issue? You need to figure that out before you go too far down the surgical path. This gets back to making sure that you have a good therapist whom you trust and are comfortable with. A correct diagnosis is absolutely critical, as you want to be able to enjoy the last quarter or third of your life. If you are doing something as significant as a gender transition, you need to do it properly.

Aging is a lot to handle for anyone: There are health issues, and people view you differently. As we age, we are not as attractive as we were when we were younger. This differential is even more evident if one transitions from male to female. An older man transitioning to a woman is never going to look like a young woman; consequently, there might need to be some mental adjustment to the picture we all carry around of how we want to look versus how we actually look. This is one of the reasons I suggested having a goal in mind but making it realistic. You want to be the best version of yourself you can be. Concerning my own transition, part of the enormous difficulty I felt during the whole process was not with the gender transition but with the age transition, and that's something that everyone has to face at some point. It is just all made more complicated when you're negotiating your new gender as well.

In addition to the psychological aspect of how you see yourself versus how people respond to you, the physical aspect of transitioning at an older age has a systemic component, and that is the status of your health, which, because of your age, may include added challenges. You may be dealing with obesity, diabetes, or even chronic pulmonary obstruction disease. These issues are a serious factor that can affect transition at a mature age. Therefore, it is critically important that when you make the decision to transition, you have a good primary-care physician on your team.

PHYSICAL CHANGES

We already talked about the effects of estrogen on your mature body. Even when using a blocker like Spironolactone, you are not going to have the results a younger person will have. However, after a few years, you should notice some nice changes in your skin, and your fat will redistribute itself. You will also be surprised at some of the benefits for your hair. When added to your regimen, Finasteride—the drug in Propecia—does help with hair growth, but not as significantly as it does in a younger person. In many cases, the hormones you take will not only make you look younger and more feminine but also help you feel better. But there is a limited effect to the hormones on a mature person's body. It seems that for every year that we get older, the hormonal influence is less. However, hormones can still make a significant change in one's demeanor even at a mature age. Some individuals find that taking estrogen balances out their emotional level, while others find that it adds serenity to their overall well-being. In fact, the discontinuance of hormones before surgery is a hotly debated issue among surgeons, because stopping the hormones can have a dramatic effect on some people's personality. Gender surgeons normally recommend stopping hormones two to three weeks ahead of surgery, but sometimes this cessation results in a patient developing great anxiety. This is not what surgeons want in their patients just before such a life-changing operation. I am not certain if the discontinuance of hormone therapy resulting in increased anxiety is completely physiological or whether there is a placebo effect with it as well. Regardless, the effects are real.

In addition to the benefits already mentioned, there are other aspects to hormone therapy that should please mature trans people. I found that the skin on my hands became thinner, and my hands now appear more like those of a natal woman, albeit a large natal woman. The fingers have become noticeably thinner, and along with a reasonable nail length, my hands suddenly appear feminine.

Another place where estrogen has had a positive effect is the shape of my legs. I wear a lot of tennis skirts, and I love to swim in the summer, and I have no hang-ups about my legs or about wearing a bathing suit. Estrogen has actually given me ankles! The change is quite remarkable.

Additionally, the estrogen has smoothed out my calf muscles, so I don't have that large bulge that men often have in their calves. Although estrogen doesn't change the length of your foot, the width can change, particularly if you are thinner than your former male self. These changes aren't mentioned very often, but I imagine you will find them pleasant developments like I did.

Another noticeable change is that of your body smell, which is significant, especially around the armpit area. The musky smell that is normally associated with men is gone. In my case, it wasn't replaced with a new scent—it just disappeared. Anyone who was a previous partner or particularly close to you physically will quickly notice this difference. Embrace it!

DENTISTRY

In addition to concern about your physical body, please consider paying some attention to your teeth. I may be biased, since I work in that area, but I am amazed at how little transgender and transsexual women take advantage of their dentist. I've mentioned this before, but cosmetic dentistry can make you look a lot more youthful and beautiful. It can also make you look more feminine. The proximal angles of women's teeth are more rounded, while men have a more squared-off shape to their teeth. I realize that good dentistry is not cheap, but taking care of your teeth should not be seen as a luxury. You should be going to your dentist for annual checkups, and you should be maintaining your dentition and maintaining your smile anyway. If you have extra money to spend on the more cosmetic aspects, take advantage of what dentistry can offer you as a woman in transition.

If your dentition needs work but finances are a challenge, I recommend going to a dental school for the required work. Dental schools do a good job, and the students and residents will create a welcoming atmosphere. But there is a difference between undergraduate students and residents. Stick with the graduate clinics. These students are postdoctoral residents who are training in specialties like periodontics (gum treatment), endodontics (root canals), and prosthodontics (full mouth reconstruction). The graduate residents perform great specialty care because they do not have the pressure of time that a practicing clinician faces each day. The only downside is that graduate clinics are more expensive than the undergraduate clinics, yet they are significantly cheaper than a specialist working in the community. Taking advantage of what dental schools can offer is a great option for someone who wants a more feminine mouth but is working with a budget.

HEALTHY LIFESTYLE

If you are thinking about going the surgical route, it is absolutely imperative that you don't smoke. Smoking delays and complicates wound healing, and most surgeons are adamant that you stop smoking before undergoing any surgical procedures. Additionally, you need to eat healthy and try to manage your lifestyle in a sensible fashion. The healthier you are prior to surgery, the easier your post-op recovery will be. Be smart; manage your body and your lifestyle.

INSURANCE AND MEDICARE

For many years, there was a lack of insurance coverage for people who wanted to medically transition. The only people who could pursue this route in a safe, professional manner were those who could pay out of pocket for their care. Then, through great work by transgender attorneys and activists representing the transgender movement, a lot of the barriers came down. We suddenly found ourselves with Article 1557 of the Affordable Care Act (ACA), which obligates insurance companies to pay for various gender reassignment procedures. Not only has there been federal support through the ACA, but in some areas of the country, there has been support at the state and city levels as well. The net result is that there is now more insurance coverage than ever before for transgender procedures. Of course, there is the possibility that some of this support may change, depending on the political climate in the country. That is why you need to be very clear about your status in terms of your insurance and what is covered and what is not covered as you start planning your transition.

A mature transitioner should also be familiar with Medicare and Medicaid and what they cover. You want to make sure you are aware of the different insurance coverages out there and what you are entitled to before you start, because when you transition at a mature age, you may be given preference by some providers, which will allow things to happen a little more quickly than you expect. It is to your advantage to be thoroughly prepared in terms of how much you may have to pay out-of-pocket for surgeries or other treatments. A good place to go for information concerning insurance coverage for gender transition is the Human Rights Campaign (hrc.org).

Again, I have mentioned many times how important it is for you to establish a relationship with a primary-care provider, be it a private practitioner or a gender clinic or hospital-based program. This is important to your overall health and is absolutely critical to your game plan and ultimate goals. So please, do not buy hormones off the street or on the Internet.

RETIREMENT

This leads me to the next issue, retirement. It is not uncommon for someone to decide to transition after they have finished their business career and are now entering retirement. They figure, "I have the time. I have some resources. I have life experience. This is a good time to transition." I think those are all salient points. But one of the biggest concerns about retirement is making sure you have enough money to last you for the rest of your life. Is the retirement a planned retirement, or is it a retirement that's been forced early because of your desire to transition? You need to evaluate your financial resources in a professional manner so that there are no surprises later. You may want to hire an accountant or an attorney to help you plan everything out. You will certainly require the services of an attorney if you end up getting a divorce. You must also ensure that you have medical insurance. Are you at the age where Medicare is now playing a role in your health care? If you have Medicare, do you have supplemental coverage? How much money do you have coming in each year, and how is that going to affect your Medicare payments each month? I realize these are not the most fun things to talk about, but they are serious issues.

The impressions and suggestions I have shared so far have been more about the physical transition, or those issues pertaining to the gender reassignment surgery process itself. I now want to share my thoughts on the more emotional or cerebral aspects of transitioning. As previously mentioned when discussing relationships, the emotional aspect of transitioning is far more difficult than the physical transformation, and I want you to be prepared, or at least to consider some of the things that I was unprepared for.

LONELINESS

When discussing a transition, many people try to support you by saying, "Well, you're going to be finally living as your 'authentic self.' It's going to be like an epiphany. It's going to be blue skies and roses." Nothing could be further from the truth. There are blue-sky days, and there are moments when you will feel incredible. But there are an awful lot of days when being a transwoman is not so great. It can be very sobering and challenging. I was very social as a man, and I continue to be very social as a woman, especially in my career. But in terms of my personal life, it is very difficult transitioning at a mature age and finding an appropriate partner. This applies whether you are looking for a same-sex partner or a partner of the opposite sex.

Transitioning at a mature age has given me the perspective of a widow, but instead of losing a spouse to death, I lost my male self completely as well as my spouse to divorce. The personal loneliness that I have experienced since my transition is far greater than I ever suspected it would be. The solitude is also more of a problem that I thought it would be. My trans self adds a barrier between other people and me, and it is hard to bridge that gap. Furthermore, I went from the luxury of being a successful, heterosexual white male to becoming a member of a seriously disenfranchised group—transgender women. Suddenly, I had to grapple with having a decreased status in the community and the potential of dramatically less earning capability in my occupation. These are only two of the many issues I could list. Sadly, there are some post-op transwomen who find that they cannot handle this dramatic change in their circumstances; therefore, I urge you to think through the long-term ramifications of fully transitioning while you still have a chance to change your mind. The only way I have been able to handle this situation is by assuming an attitude that I will not let anyone or any group "bury" me. I realize that I am fortunate in that I have a strong personality, which helps get me through the bad times, but I also feel great concern about other mature post-op trans people and their ability to navigate this maze. Support can be immensely important in helping someone adjust after their transition. I wish more spouses of transwomen could understand how isolating this situation is and provide moral support to their former (or current) spouse, even if they don't ultimately stay together. It is so needed.

The loneliness of mature post-op trans people, especially the sense of being jettisoned by society, can lead to chronic depression, which can then lead to a whole host of even more serious issues, such as suicide contemplation. This is why the offices of the surgeons performing these surgeries need to make a better attempt at staying in touch with their patients. Fortunately, I am an optimist, and have been able to avoid suicidal thoughts, but I never expected to find myself alone at this point in my life. I rarely hear the issue of elder trans loneliness discussed in a frank and public fashion. Instead, what I hear from some in the trans community is, "Oh, you're finally going to transition gender. You're going to have a great support team around you, and eventually you'll meet somebody." In some cases, yes, that's true. If you know someone who experienced their transition that way, I am really happy for them. I hope they enjoy it. But for many of us who have transitioned at a mature age, we find ourselves by ourselves. The mistake that we make is that when we transition gender and discover our authentic selves, we somehow assume that our personal lives will follow a similar path to authenticity. This is not usually the case. Even when we have a lot of friends, at the end of the day we tend to be romantically alone. The phone just doesn't ring.

Part of the problem for someone transitioning at a mature age is that we get so involved in our own physical metamorphosis that we forget about the effect on our spouses and social networks. We find ourselves becoming insanely happy with how we are changing, and we just assume that our spouses will come along for the ride. But we forget that the change, even though it is necessary for us, is only *for* us and is, in a sense, imposed on everyone else. Even if someone you are involved with thinks they understand, they can never really be part of the transition, so they are left on the outside while having their whole life change as well. Only the most patient and understanding partners make it through. For younger people, the chance of connecting with a new partner post-transition is quite good. But for the mature individual, it is a very different story.

It is even worse for trans elders who are in nursing homes or in assisted-living quarters. In those situations, trans folk who may already be estranged from their families are too often verbally abused, frequently ostracized by staff members, and generally made to feel terrible and less deserving of care. This behavior is completely reprehensible but will not change until health-care workers are exposed to more diversity training and are held accountable for their behavior toward their patients. The health-care industry needs to address this problem now!

Concerning my day-to-day existence, people in my community simply know and accept me. I conduct my life in a normal fashion, interacting with people as anyone would. I lecture at medical and dental schools, I play tennis, I fish. I do all kinds of things for work and fun, and I keep myself very busy. But I often find myself on the sidelines when my friends get together. There are a lot of activities that I do not get invited to, for one reason or another, and it stings. It also affects my ability to meet people to date, since most people meet potential partners through their friend networks if they don't do online dating. So please, be sure to factor this potential loneliness into your decision to transition. Will you be able to handle life as a "widow"? Think hard about what your life will be like post-transition.

Transitioning gender has given me a totally new respect for people who are actual widows. Being alone is a very challenging thing for these women.

FIGURE 23. Dr. Anne L. Koch, Boston, MA, 2014

This picture was taken in Boston in the fall of 2014, and I have since used it as a head-shot. I posted it on some websites as a testament to Dr. Spiegel's skills and received many wonderful compliments. I am very pleased with the results of my FFS.

I can remember many times in my previous life seeing a widow who was in her fifties and thinking, "That's so sad, but she'll be able to get back into the social scene and get on with her life." Not really. Speak to any of your female friends who are single and over fifty-five years old. They will tell you how challenging it is to be a single woman of that age, regardless of how you look. If you were a male who was sixty or seventy years old with money and a position, you will still be considered attractive. But we all know that it is not fair the way society treats women. And I mean *all* women. So, if you are transitioning to be a woman and you are over fifty-five and won't be able to keep your spouse, welcome to the world of the single older woman.

SEXUALITY AND DATING

There is so much misinformation out there on the Internet and in social media about people who transition and who subsequently have wonderful sex and dating lives. I am now starting to see some beautiful young women on YouTube who have transitioned and who have discovered that their post-surgical lives are not quite what they expected. Dating even as a young transwoman is not easy, but dating as a mature transwoman is a nightmare. Let me give you the down and dirty *from my perspective* about some things to keep in mind.

One of the problems that you have when you transition at an older age is that you are inheriting the same problems that older cisgender women are already familiar with, meaning that a lot of men who are suitably age-appropriate for you to date, if you date men, are not going to find you attractive, because older men tend to look for women who are younger than themselves. Finding a same-sex partner is sometimes easier, because women generally have a more accepting view of trans individuals, but it can still be challenging.

There is another problem that isn't commonly discussed. Let's say you fully transitioned from male to female. If you were interested in dating a straight man, then at some point you'd have to tell him that you used to be a man. But you cannot say that on the first date unless you are dating online— it's just too much information too fast. However, if you do date a man, regardless of whether you have sexual activity or not, certainly by the third date you need to break the story. As a transwoman, when you inform a heterosexual man that you used to be a man, your first concern should always be for your physical safety. You don't want to be assaulted—or worse. So, you have to be very careful in choosing a man to date. But when you tell a man your story, even if you think he can handle it, it must be done in a certain way. My experience is that none of them can handle it. But if you tell a straight guy that you used to be a man and they seemingly *can* handle it, you still have another problem. They have leverage over you for the remainder of your relationship, because every time you fight, it will always come up, "Well, you know, Annie, you're not a real woman." This is a hurtful thing to say, and it will be trotted out again and again to score points. Transwomen are women, in my opinion, and deserve to be treated with respect, so I don't want to hear it. I don't like it when people have leverage over me in my business life, and I certainly don't want it in my personal life.

If there is a man who comes along who is attracted to me because of the fact that I am a transwoman, I personally wonder about that guy. When I was in Japan, I dated transsexual women, not only because they were attractive but also because I saw a bit of myself in them. Those transsexual women in Japan (new half) were very attuned to men who found them attractive. And for years there has been a saying in the trans community, "Show me a guy who finds a tranny attractive and I'll show you a tranny." I know there will be some people who argue that point and say that not everyone who dates transwomen wants to be a transwoman. This is mostly from younger individuals who don't have as much experience and want to believe the best of people. But in many instances, it has been my experience that men who find transwomen attractive often have the yearning to be like us themselves.

On the other hand, women can be incredible romantic partners, not just due to their physical attributes but also as a result of their open-minded mentality. Many women can look past a trans person's physicality and concentrate more on their personality. This is greatly appreciated by any trans person. While I do find most women attractive, I do find there can be serious problems with dating them as well. The main problem is that women, like men, can hold as leverage against us the fact that we were not physically born as women.

Another challenge for some transwomen is that dating a woman places you in the category of now having a lesbian identity in the eyes of society. Women who date women are seen a certain way, so this is something that a transwoman who is interested in dating women must adjust to as well. This huge second switch in identity might be a problem for a transwoman who was previously in a long-term heterosexual relationship.

So, at the end of the day, what do we have in terms of our dating life? Perhaps the only person who can truly understand me is another transwoman. But am I attracted to transwomen? Basically, I am open to dating anyone I seem to have a connection with. Like everyone else, I am looking for somebody to love. Furthermore, it doesn't matter at this point in my life whether it's a cisgender guy, a cisgender woman, or a trans woman, as long as it's the same species! I am looking for somebody I can connect with on an emotional level. It's just that as I am getting back into the dating scene, I find the landscape so challenging. Have I tried online dating as a transwoman? No, because I have a few friends who have had nightmare experiences. Of course, a few have hit home runs, so perhaps I will eventually try that route. But in the meantime, I'm trying to be the best person I can be, with a unique perspective that I think could be attractive and fulfilling to a partner. But for those of you thinking about your transition, please understand that your social and romantic life going forward is going to be a challenge, especially if you've found yourself alone after years of being in a committed relationship.

SEXUAL SATISFACTION

Generally, when surgeons and other medical providers involved in transgender health care discuss a vaginoplasty procedure, they talk about how the patient will still have the ability to orgasm. However, I believe that this result is overhyped in order to calm people's fears. Just the taking of estrogen, along with the reduction in testosterone following the removal of the testes, knocks down one's libido. Concerning your sensate clitoris, it's probably not going to be anywhere near as sensitive as you may hope. The natal clitoris has significantly more nerve endings than the glans penis. When gender surgeons perform vaginoplasty surgeries, they dramatically reduce the size of the glans penis, and they use that material to create a neo-clitoris, but it's a clitoris with a lot less sensitivity. If you are lucky, there will be other aspects of the sexual encounter that will contribute to your ability to orgasm. If you are transitioning at a mature age, don't go into the experience expecting that you are going to become this incredibly sexy, orgasmic individual. If you do, honey, good for you! But regardless of who does your surgery, I think you are going

FIGURE 24. Relaxing at Club, Cape Cod, MA, 2015
This is the real Anne Koch relaxing on Cape Cod. I enjoy my life as a woman, and
I am very pleased to be accepted as such. Developing self-confidence is so important
for anyone who transitions. This is particularly true for mature individuals.

to find yourself in a place where it is going to require a lot of effort. It may, in fact, take a few years before you find the formula that allows you to get off. However, this is a case-by-case basis, and at an older age, especially as a woman, having an orgasm is very different from a man's experience. There is a lot more that goes into our satisfaction of sex as a woman. For me, the good news is that since I had my revision surgery, I am a lot more sensitive down below. I did not expect this, and it is a much-welcomed change.

In actuality, I am still trying to figure out exactly where I am on the sexual scale. This confusion is something many trans people experience, as our worlds get all shaken up. As a man, I was definitely heterosexual; I never had any homosexual urges. My real pleasure was satisfying my female partner. Oral sex, especially giving oral sex, was something that was probably my greatest enjoyment. But now, as a transsexual woman, I still enjoy that, but it is not so easy finding an appropriate partner. Actually, I find it very difficult, as I mentioned in the section on dating. But I also really enjoy my life as a woman. I also enjoy the "straight world," if you want to call it that. For the first time, I now find men attractive. I see men in a different manner than how I viewed them for the first sixty-five years of my life. Where my personal journey will end up, I don't know. But I am looking for somebody who is simpatico on more than just a physical level. I want someone to share my life and my aspirations with, to enjoy the rest of my life with. I'm also looking for someone whose career I can help, someone I can support. This is a big deal for me. Otherwise, I'm basically a happy girl. Would I love to find an over-the-moon-and-back love affair? Sure—I would love to be in love with someone in such a deep way. Realistically, I think that is very unlikely at this point in my life, but I will continue to try to find it. I hope that everyone reading this book will continue to try to reach that goal for themselves.

SELF-ESTEEM

I would like to further discuss the hurtful idea that transwomen are not "real" women. For someone to use that as leverage against us is disappointing, but it is prevalent in both the straight and the gay worlds, and I hate that. Unfortunately, there's very little that we can do about it other than guard against it and bring public awareness to the issue. I know that I will never be exactly like a natural-born physical woman, but I am still a woman. You must understand and internalize this as well. I have always felt like a woman inside, and because of my complicated life story, I have certain aspects to my personality and my essence that give me a unique perspective. How many people have had a chance to experience life both as a man and as a woman? So, the ignorance and cruelty of others doesn't destroy me, but it does disappoint me that my status can be used as leverage against me by both men and women. In fact, it can lead to abusive relationships. To discuss these issues truthfully, out in the open, is why I lecture at schools and organizations. I am looking for and representing the truth. There is a large amount of misinformation that trans people must go through in our quest to reach the truth about what transitioning is really like and whether our reality will match the fantasy. There are so many issues that go under the "transgender" umbrella now. I think it is very important for the medical community, including social workers and therapists, to start sorting things out. It is incumbent upon them to separate the truth from the politically convenient for the sake of their patients.

POLITICAL CORRECTNESS

Political correctness creates a lot of problems for people entering the transgender community. The media teaches us that we need to support people's life choices, and that if someone says they're transgender, then we must accept that and support them no matter what. And if they are truly transgender, then yes, we should be staunch supporters. However, there are presently "transgender people" who might not be truly gender dysphoric. They seem to be following a trend, whether because they know someone else who is transitioning or because they've seen it on TV or for some other reason entirely. They might feel that they are different from everyone else, and might just assume that their mis-assigned gender is to blame. It is hard to tell, though—a person can have other health issues that overlap and intersect, similar to the Olympic rings. These conditions may mimic some of the feelings or desires of the truly gender dysphoric. That is why it is so critical that you get professional help to determine what the real story is in your case. Are you truly gender dysphoric, or are you somewhere along a different spectrum? These questions are about your own health. Because you're transitioning at a mature age, it is even more critical that the diagnosis be correct and be based not on political correctness or trendiness but on medical facts. Please be vigilant in how you go about determining who you truly are and what you want to do. It is so important.

For years, the idea of changing gender has been driven through material posted on the Internet. There are websites geared toward the trans experience from many different angles, and every day there is more material posted. Yes, there is some very good, useful information on the web. However, misinformation and character assassination appears daily, and this mix of reliable and suspicious information has now branched out into social media. All kinds of people espouse their viewpoints on the Internet as if they were experts. They may know nothing, but by calling themselves a blogger or an activist, they assume the mantle of respectability and expertise. It is important to ask yourself what kind of background these "experts" have. As I have discovered through my own journey, when we transition, we are all grasping for straws. We are desperate for information, particularly for information that validates what we already think. You must be so careful as you go forward through your transition not to be duped. With the current political climate in the United States, people are going into their own ghettos, where all they see is their own viewpoint. Rather than just having people echo what you already think, you must be able to seek out other viewpoints in order to get a better understanding of the situation. That is the only way we can make informed, intelligent decisions.

THE WOMAN I HAVE BECOME

I have just shared various impressions from my own transition process and would now like to share some of the experiences that have contributed to me becoming the woman I am today. When you transition, you can continue to enjoy everything that you enjoyed as a man. A good place to begin is with women's athletics. I personally hated the men's locker room when I was a jock. Taking a shower with all the other men was so uncomfortable for me, and I always tried to find a way to take a shower without being in the presence of other guys. Boys and men have a habit of parading around nude and comparing their "anatomy." Although I was an exceptional athlete, I had a relatively small penis, so the whole locker room culture of strutting around and comparing one's dick size was appalling to me. The combination of being uncomfortable in the men's locker room along with my awareness that my feeling like a woman was never going to go away is what made me completely walk away from sports. I am thrilled that at this point in my life I can now enjoy being a female athlete and feel comfortable in the women's locker room. I no longer have a fear of taking a shower in the presence of others, and women certainly don't go around parading their anatomy. I feel much more at home there. Sometimes I will be sitting around in the women's locker room after a game of tennis and a woman will approach me and ask, "Annie, do you have a couple of minutes to talk?" and then will ask me business questions. I love giving advice to my female friends about what they want to do in such an informal atmosphere. The fact that I'm accepted there reinforces my feeling of rightness—I am a woman, and therefore, I'm much more at home in the women's locker room.

I lead my life 24/7 as a woman. I don't go around announcing to people, "Hi, I'm Anne Koch. I'm a transwoman." I simply say, "Hi, I'm Anne Koch." If somebody knows about my past, I don't mind. If someone has seen me speak at a medical school or seen me at some other conference, that's fine. I am happy to talk about what it's like to be a transwoman. But the majority of the time, people just see me as Anne Koch, a tall, blonde woman, and I lead my life as such. But leading my life as a woman is so different from leading my life as a man, especially when it comes to the genitalia. It is very different having a vagina, especially one that requires maintenance. To me, it is wonderful. At times, I find myself looking at my naked body in the full-length mirror. I am just so thrilled to see what I have—and what I *don't* have. Female genitalia are beautiful. I have also been introduced to things I didn't know existed before. Things like panty liners, because if you go the surgical route down below, you will have lubrication that keeps your genitalia moist. But it can also soil your underwear. I do not enjoy wearing panty liners, but I've ruined a fair amount of panties, so I've learned to get used to it.

Another thing about becoming a woman is that you become a member of "the short urethra club." Surgeons remove four to five inches of the male urethra when performing gender reassignment surgery. The difference is noteworthy, especially as a mature individual. Men have better control of their urethra and don't "leak." Also, men can stop urinating mid-flow very easily, but for a woman, when it starts to flow, it comes out quickly. Of course, I would be remiss if I did not mention the greater possibility of getting an infection with a shorter urethra—all part of becoming a woman.

FIGURE 25. Tennis is a passion, Cape Cod, MA, 2015
Tennis is a passion for me, and one of the greatest aspects of my transition has been
my participation in sports as a female athlete. I love it, and my recommendation for
anyone who transitions is to continue to do what you enjoy.

As I became more comfortable in my female identity, I discovered that I really needed at least one good girlfriend. This was important to me because we all have our self-doubts and our insecurities, and it is nice to spend time with girlfriends who can boost you up when you need it. Women are great at being nurturing—that is one of the great things I found out after transitioning. In addition to being able to enjoy playing sports again as a woman, I discovered how utterly fabulous a girls' night out is. You get a couple of women together, and you go out to dinner or to a bar, and it is so much fun. Every few months, my girlfriends and I need to have a girls' night out, and we meet at some local restaurant. For myself, a very significant part of being a woman is enjoying camaraderie with other women. It makes me feel like I belong and keeps me in touch with my friends. Furthermore, having a group of women friends who want to hang out with me regularly helps validate my decision to transition at age sixty-three . . . for myself!

Another significant aspect of transitioning from male to female is the ingestion of estrogen. The effect of taking estrogen for an XY individual expresses itself in different ways. Some transwomen become very susceptible to crying jags, while others seem more prone to stress and anxiety. Others may find themselves gaining weight in an alarming fashion. While I did not suffer from crying jags or greatly increased anxiety, I did experience some changes as a result of hormone administration. People always ask me if I find that I'm more emotional because of the hormones, but the truth is, I do not think my essential nature has changed much at all. The biggest change was the ability to express my emotions openly, which is so different from my experience as a man—and I like it.

A good example of this was the passing of my best friend, John Scott, and how it still affects me to this day. John and I were best friends from third grade all the way up until his death. Although we had very different interests (mine was sports, his was electronics), this difference allowed us to forge a noncompetitive bond. As teenagers and young adults, we shared everything with each other. Our dating life with girlfriends, our future goals and aspirations, our insecurities . . . everything. Life happens, and we went our separate ways, but when I returned to Long Island in 2003, we reconnected in the best way. We became fishing buddies, and he loved fishing with me because I had been a professional and always caught and released a lot of fish. We shared so many wonderful times together on my boat. This all came to an end when he was diagnosed with prostate cancer. Most men do well with treatment for prostate cancer, but John's cancer quickly metastasized to other parts of his body, and within eight months, he went from 175 pounds to 89 pounds.

I remember very well my last visit to see him in hospice. He was having a lot of difficulty eating, and he described the mere attempt as being "like pouring gravel down my throat." I brought him a Carvel chocolate thick shake float (made with soft ice cream), the same kind I had brought for my father in his final days. Incredibly, John was able to drink this, and even more amazingly, he enjoyed it! After the shake, we talked for a while and I leaned down and held his hand, kissed him on the cheek, and told him, "John, you were the best friend I could ever possibly have wanted." I started to cry, and he said the same thing to me; then we both hugged and cried.

Soon after, I said goodbye to his wife and left. I knew it would be the last time I would see my best friend, and in fact, he died two days later. Whenever I think about this, it is profoundly emotional for me. I still cry about his death, and I cried as I wrote this. But I am so happy that I can now freely share something that was so meaningful to me—and share it without any shame.

In addition to my newfound ability to share my emotions, I now find myself being more tolerant of those who disagree with me than I was when I was a man. I don't know whether it is the estrogen or the simple fact of getting old. It is most likely a combination of both, but I do find my current personality to be an amalgamation of all my life experiences.

THE DOWNSIDE OF BEING A WOMAN

There are other aspects of living as a woman that are different from those of a man and that, unfortunately, are not so joyful. For instance, I will never forget the first time that I was walking down a street in Boston, late at night, and heard footsteps behind me. This was a non-event for the first sixty-three years of my life, but after I transitioned, walking down a city street late at night and someone comes around a corner and you hear footsteps behind you . . . that was a very scary experience. Suddenly, I realized how alone and vulnerable I was to harassment, attack, or something worse. Women have a seasoned vigilance that men don't, which they learn when they are very young. Sadly, this is part of the socialization process. So now, if I'm walking down a street and I hear footsteps behind me, I don't dare turn around and look at them as if I were in a horror movie. But I do start looking in the windows of adjacent buildings to try to see who is behind me. What are they doing? Are they walking faster? Do they seem threatening? As a woman, it is just something that you have to be aware of.

Being able to get back into my profession and get re-established as a woman puts me, very sadly, in a very small percentage of trans people. Many trans people are not able to return to their previous occupation or specialty because of extreme bias in their industry. But going back into the professional world of dental medicine and surgery has given me an entirely new perspective. It is much more difficult getting things done as a woman. The difference is profound, and as an individual who has been on both sides of the ledger, this makes no sense to me. I am also stunned that even in this day and age, some men feel as if they can summarily dismiss me. This kind of response is something you must factor in when contemplating a change of gender at a mature age. Will you be able to handle this change in how people relate to you, or will it have a devastating effect on you?

Another thing I have learned is how quick men are to take credit for things that women have created. The first time this happened to me, I was extremely taken aback. It had never occurred to me that such a thing could happen! I quickly developed a response that would not seem threatening or unprofessional but would be firm. From having lived sixty-three years as a male, I know that this reaction is not necessarily a cognitive process for men; they merely see it as part of their God-given right of possessing a Y chromosome. They have been socialized to accept that men always have primacy. But I do respond to this type of behavior and call men out on it. I think all women should push back against men who dismiss their achievements or try to take credit for their work. However, I realize that I am in a position where I may be able to respond in such a way because of my status, whereas other women may not feel comfortable responding in a similar fashion. I am trying to make a difference here and become a leader among women in my specialty. It's a work in progress.

I have also found that as a woman, the pressure to conform to certain ideals and behavior far exceeds those expectations placed on men. Things don't seem to be getting better in how society perceives women. Multiple times I have had women approach me after lectures and ask, "Why would I ever want to become a woman when it is so much easier being a man?" I explain to them that there really wasn't a choice in my case, but that question nevertheless haunts me.

9 · REALITY, MYTHS, AND THE FUTURE OF TRANSGENDER HEALTH CARE

TRANSGENDER MEDICINE AND SURGERY IN THE FUTURE

The whole spectrum of transgender health care itself is very fluid. Going forward, the landscape of transgender medicine will look very different as more doctors start treating trans patients and as advances are made in all areas of trans medical care. In this chapter, I offer my thoughts about future changes in transgender health care as well as share my hopes. I also expose some myths commonly encountered during a transition. But let's first examine some potential changes in transgender health care and the way services will be delivered.

Going forward, we will see the creation of more university- and hospital-based transgender medicine and surgery programs. Many of these programs will have a teaching component, so we can anticipate the creation of more fellowships in transgender surgery and transgender psychiatric medicine. Mount Sinai Hospital in New York City was the first in the United States to establish such programs, and it is to be commended for such action. Actually, Scandinavian countries did this years ago, and they found that the delivery of transgender surgical care through academic medical centers resulted in the surgeons becoming much faster in their surgical time. Additionally, the complication rate following these procedures dropped off significantly. This makes so much sense. If, as a surgeon, you are concentrating on a specific technique, your speed will increase as you master that technique, and you will have far fewer complications. More specifically, in their superb article studying male-to-female gender reassignment surgery over fourteen years, Sigurjónsson et al. note, "Our surgical experience from treating MtF transsexual patients for over fourteen years shows that GRS (gender reassignment surgery) has been a viable and safe procedure for an increasing number of patients. During the study period, there was a significant reduction found in the operating time and is now comparatively short with maintained low rates of reoperations. This suggests that GRS surgery should be performed at few centres so that surgical experience and volume may be optimized."[1]

Further validation of these conclusions can be seen by examining the operation time required for the procedure: "The length of surgery has steadily decreased with experience from 200–250 minutes 10–15 years ago to under 120 min for the year 2013" (which was the last year in the study). Additionally, this study examined complications, and its findings "were similar in type and frequency to that of other centres." Some of the complications included postoperative bleeding at 11 percent and wound infection at 10 percent. Also, the serious issue of a rectovaginal fistula was found to be 2 percent. These complication rates were quite reasonable for the surgeries performed.

Complications involved in gender reassignment surgery are factors with which all potential patients must become familiar. In their recent article on the complications related to the neovagina in male-to-female transgender surgery, Dreher et al. report on the surgical results of 1,684 patients. They discovered a complication rate of 32.5 percent and a reoperation rate of 21.7 percent for non-aesthetic reasons.[2] The most common complication was stenosis of the neo-meatus, which refers to a narrowing or stricture of the new urethra opening. Postoperative bleeding problems, if they occur, are commonly associated with the urethra.

In an article published in the March 2018 issue of the *Journal of Urology*, Gaither et al. review the records of 330 male-to-female patients who presented for penile inversion vaginoplasty with a high-volume surgeon. "Of the patients, 95 (28.7%) presented with a postoperative complication. Median time to a complication was 4.4 months. Rectovaginal fistulas developed in 3 patients (0.9%)."[3] Interestingly, a fairly consistent complication rate of between 28 and 33 percent can be implied from these larger studies, a rate that is significantly greater than the one in the Sigurjónsson et al. article.

Although the complication rate associated with a vaginoplasty is dramatically lower than the complication rate associated with a phalloplasty, a patient should always be aware that complications can and will occur. Surgery should not be entered into cavalierly, and positive outcomes should certainly not be considered a given. Surgery is serious business.

Reviewing the literature, the incidence of a rectovaginal fistula seems to be in the 1 to 2 percent range. However, I've spoken with surgeons off the record, and it seems that the rate of such a complication may be slightly higher. Regardless of the seemingly low rate, a rectovaginal fistula can be a serious complication of GRS. When advising patients, some surgeons may be reluctant to admit that this complication can occur, but since there is always a small chance you will be among that number, you should be aware of the risk.

In the near future, in addition to seeing more university- and hospital-based programs, we can expect to see more providers across the board working in transgender medicine. This is not limited to surgery but includes primary care and associated specialties, such as endocrinology and psychiatric medicine. We have already started to see this trend, and I expect far more women to enter the field of transgender medicine than we currently see practicing. I have personally witnessed the more positive and nurturing attitude that natal women bring into their treatment space, particularly as it relates to improved follow-up care. Additionally, there will be more providers becoming trained in transgender medicine. Both of these are welcome changes, since it means better patient care for people undergoing GRS.

It seems fairly obvious to me that undergoing gender reassignment surgery won't "cure" gender dysphoria. It is a much more complicated issue than can be resolved simply by a surgical procedure. In their 2017 article reporting on the quality of life of transgender women, Lindquist et al. show that "transgender women reported a lower quality of life, both physical and mental health, than the general population. Although surgical treatment led to an initial trend towards improved quality of life, this decreased with time (up to five years)." Most important was the conclusion of the study: "The major finding of clinical importance is the poor quality of life reported by transgender women compared to the general population, confirming the vulnerability of this population and underlining the need for appropriate care and treatment."[4]

In her classic 2011 paper, which is often misinterpreted by anti-trans folks, Cecilia Dhejne et al. concludes, "This study found substantially higher rates of overall mortality, death from cardiovascular disease and suicide, suicide attempts, and psychiatric hospitalizations in sex-reassigned transsexual individuals compared to a healthy control population. This highlights that post-surgical transsexuals are a risk group that need long-term psychiatric and somatic follow-up. Even though surgery and hormonal therapy alleviates gender dysphoria, it is apparently not sufficient to remedy the high rates of morbidity and mortality found among transsexual persons. Improved care for the transsexual group after the sex reassignment should therefore be considered."[5]

This research underscores what I've been relating anecdotally and through my own story: don't go into your transition thinking that surgery is going to solve all your problems. There is actual research to show that this will most likely not be the case. Do yourself a favor by taking the time to set up your support network ahead of time, as I've outlined in this book. I was shocked and confused to find that after my vaginoplasty, I was completely on my own. Fortunately, I was able to overcome the obstacles, but I simply could not believe the complete lack of follow-up care from my doctor. I even tried reaching out to my therapist, but I did not receive any response. While there's the predictable initial euphoria after undergoing GRS, certainly by the second post-op year, a patient can get the feeling of being lost or completely abandoned. It is so important that the medical community establishes a continuity of care and does some follow-up with GRS patients. This should be a multidiscipline approach across medical specialties.

In his dissertation on outcomes and refinements of GRS, Dr. Hannes Sigurjónsson concludes, "When compared to the general population, transgender women report a lower quality of life (QoL). Surgical treatment has the possibility to relieve gender dysphoria and thereby raise QoL. However, this improvement shows a trend to decline over time. This confirms the vulnerability of the transgender population and emphasizes the need for suitable care both before and after GCS."[6]

In order to train all those providers who will eventually be moving into transgender medicine, we will see more medical centers develop continuing medical education courses for providers. Primary-care providers, including physician assistants and nurse practitioners, will be increasingly targeted for training. Most people in transgender medicine understand the wisdom of a multidiscipline approach, so it makes sense for more people to be adequately trained.

Over the next three to five years, I expect the recent rapid growth of transgender patients requesting surgical services to slow down. I believe this will be a result of more people who talk honestly about the myriad challenges associated with a full surgical transition, along with declining media interest as transitioning becomes more normalized. The sensational aspect of changing one's gender will hopefully be replaced with more focus on getting better outcomes from the procedures being performed. My feeling is that rather than full transitions, we will see more requests of a gender nonconforming nature. Already we are seeing patients request "a little testosterone" or hormone administration "to become a little feminine." Some patients are even requesting other surgical procedures. The line between legitimate surgical intervention and body modification may become increasingly blurred. Consequently, the surgical demand will remain high but will increase at a slower rate. There will also be far more surgeons providing services.

In terms of procedures themselves, I expect to see an increased demand for zero-depth vaginoplasty, or what Dr. Sidhbh Gallagher refers to as a "dimple vaginoplasty," along with increased demand for drain-free top surgery for transgender men. Transmen who undergo double mastectomies routinely have drains placed in their chest following the procedure. These drains, which are removed when the patient is healed, have the potential to get infected and leave some scarring. Dr. Gallagher does a drain-free procedure that requires minimal maintenance, and her postoperative results are excellent, with seemingly less scarring. Needless to say, her patients are thrilled. I fully expect other surgeons to investigate this technique.

A dimple vaginoplasty, on the other hand, accomplishes the goal for the patient of having female-appearing external genitalia but does not create a vaginal canal. This option is attractive to those individuals who have no interest in penetrative sex and do not want the burden of dilating for the rest of their life. We will also see an increased interest in pelvic physical therapy for post-op transwomen, as well as renewed interest in a hybrid or two-stage approach for vaginoplasty procedures.

Concerning pelvic physical therapy, Dr. Gallagher writes:

These are physical therapists who have special qualifications and certifications and really just specialize in the pelvic floor. As you know, your new vagina, like any vagina, is made to travel through the vaginal hiatus, which is basically a channel that goes through your pelvic floor. The pelvic floor is essentially a sheet of muscle, and the better control you have over it the better you will be able to use and enjoy your new vagina. The therapists bring a lot of expertise in areas such as incontinence, sexual function, and they are experts in dilation, which of course is so important for the vaginoplasty patients.[7]

As I've described in other chapters, a two-visit or hybrid stage vaginoplasty means that the patient is informed before treatment that after the initial procedure, at approximately the three- to six-month point post-surgery, they will need to return and have the genital aesthetics tweaked along with any other physiologic issues. Regarding this procedure, Dr. Sigurjónsson and colleagues write,

> Surgery was performed largely as described in the literature, with solely penile skin for the vaginal lining using the penile inversion technique. After 6–12 months, we did a second-stage procedure with the creation of the clitoral hood and inner labia along with cutting of the posterior commissure. [The posterior commissure is the place where the labia meet in the back, and cutting this improves aesthetics and allows for easier sexual penetration.] The two-stage technique used by us and other centres holds several advantages to a one-stage surgical protocol. In brief, a minor second-stage surgical session gives [the surgeon] good control of the final outcome, as the healing after the first stage is complete with scarring and symmetry accurately determined and treated. The second stage also allows for avoiding intravaginal skin grafts in many patients, which would not be possible in a single-stage protocol due to the temporarily deformed introitus caused by the significant stretching of the skin. ["Introitus" refers to the opening leading to the vaginal canal. A two-stage procedure allows the body to heal after the initial surgery so that the surgeon can go back later and fine-tune the aesthetics to make the vulva more natural looking after the surgical site has settled down.] We offer single-stage surgery to selected patients but avoid this if at all possible as we believe a two-stage protocol offers a better long-term outcome.

They continue, "A two-stage surgery could be an advantage in the path to succeed in an aesthetically pleasing outcome, as patients and surgeons have been increasingly focused on [the] aesthetic outcome of GRS in the past years."[8] Given my own experience, I agree wholeheartedly that the two-stage procedure is preferable, and I wish I'd been offered that option.

In addition to these various clinical issues, I fully anticipate a more robust discussion in the medical community concerning the ethics of transgender medicine. While many positive accomplishments for GRS have certainly been achieved for the transgender community, we are now in the throes of an ethical dilemma in transgender medicine. Currently, there are some surgeons who are driven into the field of trans medicine for the financial gain and who are performing significant numbers of operations on very young patients. Of course, there are many physicians with an honest desire to be supportive of their patients, particularly the young ones. Nevertheless, genital surgery on patients less than eighteen years of age remains a challenging and controversial area of transgender medicine. This is principally due to the lack of long-term evidence-based studies on this group. Simultaneously, there are some academic medical researchers who see transgender medicine as an opportunity to gain promotion within their respective academic institutions. The goal of many academics is to move from assistant professor to associate professor or to move from associate to full professor status. Transgender medicine is too rich of a target to ignore, with its potential for research articles. But who is looking out for the patient?

It is so easy to game the system in transgender medicine, both as a patient and as a provider. As a patient, it is very easy to go to the Internet and learn all the "correct answers" that will get you what you want from parents, therapists, and doctors. This reminds me of my military draft days, when we would research prepared answers to the army's medical questions that would hopefully defer us from being inducted at the time of our physical examination.

It is also easy for providers to game the system. For example, surgeons may have "feeder therapists," who send them a continuous flow of patients already debriefed and ready for surgical intervention. My concern is whether the psychiatric care offered to these patients is thorough and tailored to the specific patient, or whether it is just seen as a formality by both the patient and the therapist toward a foregone conclusion. I know the politically correct answer to that question, but I wonder what the real answer is.

I have also noticed that some health-care professionals worry about being labeled "transphobic" or having their reputations smeared on the Internet if they should ever say no to a patient's request for GRS, regardless of the age of the patient. I fully understand their concern. Anonymous online attacks can ruin careers without leaving any room for the physicians to defend themselves. Outside the casual political argument about online bullying, though, my worry is that medical decisions are being made by providers who are driven more by political expediency than by an actual patient-based approach. This is where the ethical dilemma becomes very real.

A 2018 article in the *Washington Post* addressing the controversies surrounding adolescents and gender dysphoria references University of California, San Francisco, clinical psychologist Erica Anderson, a transgender woman who transitioned late in life: "'I think a fair number of kids are getting into it [transitioning] because it's trendy,' said Anderson, who was married for thirty years and fathered two children before transitioning seven years ago. Dr. Anderson continues, 'I'm often the naysayer at our meetings. I'm not sure it's [the problem of the adolescent that she is counseling] always really [that they are] trans. I think in our haste to be supportive, we're missing that element. Kids are all about being accepted by their peers. It's trendy for professionals too.'"[9]

In the abstract from his article on the ethical concerns of treating gender dysphoria, Dr. Stephen B. Levine writes, "There is a distinct difference between pronouncements that represent human rights ideals and the reality of clinical observations. Some interpret this clash as a moral issue. This article delves into these tensions and reminds apologists from both passionate camps that clinical science has a rich tradition of resolving controversy through careful follow-up, which is not yet well developed in this arena."[10]

Furthermore, British psychotherapist James Caspian, who has extensive experience working with transgender patients, notes, "We need to be able to discuss this serious business of gender transition by gathering research and listening to clinicians." But, as Caspian says, "Too many clinicians are afraid of speaking up." He continues, "One clinician told me she felt like a heretic, another said that, 'I didn't think we were allowed to talk about this detransitioning.' They are afraid for their careers."[11]

I have no interest in getting into an intense political discussion here about whether or not it is right for teens to have GRS based on their age. My point is that going forward, patient decisions need to be made based on *clinical evaluation*, not on what is politically expedient. This applies to patients of *all* ages. We need to make our practices patient based, and we need to establish a follow-up protocol and a continuity of care for these patients. Transgender medicine has come so far so quickly that bumps are to be expected. I fully expect my medical colleagues to get this right as we go forward, but there will continue to be challenges as the field develops.

One challenging area still to be grappled with is what to do about fees and insurance coverage. Many physicians equate transgender medicine with bariatric medicine years ago. As more physicians became trained in that specialty, fees decreased as access to care increased. This may occur in transgender medicine as well, especially as more surgeons emerge from the newer training centers, but insurance coverage for patients will probably also play a significant role. The more people who have insurance that covers GRS, the more people there will be who can afford to opt for the surgery. Regardless of this, though, there will continue to be private practices that will not accept insurance.

Future insurance coverage, including Medicare and Medicaid, will be, as always in the United States, subject to the winds of political change. It seems likely that insurance coverage will be delegated according to individual state regulations. And federal regulations against gender identity discrimination seem likely to be challenged in the current political atmosphere. As Kellan E. Baker mentions writes, "Section 1557 of the Affordable Care Act bans discrimination on the basis of sex, and in May 2016, HHS issued a regulation interpreting this provision as encompassing discrimination based on gender identity." He concludes his article on a positive note, "Transgender people's need for care that affirms their true selves and promotes their health and well-being parallels all Americans' desire for high-quality, affordable health insurance coverage and health care. As assaults on nondiscrimination protections for transgender people and attacks on the ACA continue, critical federal protections should be defended at all costs. But regardless of the outcome of these battles, I believe the wave of positive change transforming transgender Americans' access to health insurance and care will continue to grow."[12]

TRANS WISH LIST FOR THE FUTURE

At this point, I'd like to share my hopes for the future state of transgender medicine. First, I want transgender medicine and transgender surgery to become accepted as a legitimate part of medicine. It is a professional goal of mine to have transgender health care become part of the medical and dental school curriculum. There has been significant progress toward this acceptance, but there is still more work to be done. As more medical schools and hospitals recognize transgender medicine, and as more of these institutions create formal training programs, the legitimacy of transgender health care will become established.

My second wish dovetails the first. There must be more evidence-based research in transgender health care. Most research in transgender medicine has been what we call "consensus based," with implied results—for example, studying the HIV rate among transgender sex workers in a particular city or country. Yes, this is important work, but I feel that we need more evidence-based studies related to regular transgender surgical intervention, such as those addressing questions like, How many people are thinking of committing suicide five years after having GRS, and then ten years out? Does the success of gender reassignment surgery have any relationship to age? What is the quality of life for the patient after undergoing gender reassignment surgery? Most importantly, we need to evaluate transgender studies with the same critical eye we evaluate research in other fields of medicine.

For example, there was a recent study published by Dr. Jochen Hess at University Hospital, Essen, Germany. This study followed 156 patients who surgically transitioned from male to female over a twenty-year period. After gender reassignment surgery, 75 percent of respondents reported an improvement in their quality of life, 67 percent were satisfied with their appearance as a woman, and 80 percent perceived themselves as women. Furthermore, 76.2 percent reported that they were capable of having an orgasm.[13] This study has become heavily promoted on the Internet as validating GRS, but let's take a closer look at the results.

In my specialty, endodontics, a ten-year success rate is generally 96 to 97 percent. If you are a practicing endodontic specialist and your success rate is only 90 percent, you are doing something wrong. A 10 percent failure rate is not acceptable. Yet in this study of transgender medicine, a 25 percent failure rate (quality of life not improved) is deemed acceptable. Is it really? Also, 33 percent of the respondents are *not* pleased with their appearance, and nearly 24 percent are not capable of achieving orgasm. We can do better, and we need to do better.

Furthermore, the study has serious limitations. University Hospital identified over 600 patients between 1995 and 2015, yet only 156 were included in the study. Others could not be located or did not respond to inquiries by the hospital. Consequently, 156 respondents represent just over 25 percent of the total number of patients. So, how pleased do you think the other 75 percent were with their results? Generally, it has been my experience that people who participate in studies are pleased with their outcomes, although this is an obvious generalization. The point that I am making is that there is a strong possibility that the results are not even as good as reported. My criticism is not with Dr. Hess or University Hospital. I have great respect for them, and I am completely supportive of any medical colleagues who are making a serious attempt to improve the quality of life for transgender patients. They should be commended for that. But I want to see transgender studies evaluated with the same critical eye that we evaluate research in other specialties. I want the bar in transgender medicine to be as high as it is in any other discipline. If the results are not as good as they should be, how can the medical community make them better? Do doctors need to improve their patient selection process? Should there be a more proactive system of follow-up to surgery cases? Do we need a central data-collection agency? Instituting this kind of rigorous inquiry and evaluation is how transgender medicine will reach legitimacy, not by the Internet gushing over the modest results of one study.

Another example of research that is needed concerns patients under twenty years old who have undergone gender reassignment surgery. Three or five years post-surgery, what is their level of satisfaction with their life? How is their physical and mental health? We should also investigate how many young transsexual women in their first year of college, or those directly out of high school, have lost significant depth and width of their neovagina from lack of dilation. Dilating is such an important aspect of trans health, as I mentioned earlier, and if you are a young trans woman, I think taking a gap year after high school to make your transition is smart. You need to heal from all the procedures, and you need to be diligent with the dilation; plus, it will give you some time to get used to your new life. But there should be at least one evidence-based study on how these young women are doing based on the care they received. Do young women who have the procedure done between high school and college really lose significant neovaginal depth? This is very important to investigate, because going back and re-establishing depth is hard for the surgeon who is going to be doing that procedure, and if we knew where the breakdown in care happened, the industry could adjust its methods to address that.

While I wish that there were fewer surgeries being done on teenage patients, I firmly believe that there are some young patients for whom the surgical route is absolutely the proper decision. There just seems to be so many young people being pegged for surgery lately that I think doctors should slow down a bit and re-examine their diagnoses. I also wish there was a more deliberate way of making patient selection in the first place. Overall, I think patient selection in transgender medicine needs to be improved. Along with a lack of continuity of care, patient selection is one of the most important areas in the field that needs attention.

And even though I want doctors to be conservative in their diagnoses, I also wish that cis physicians were more accepting of gender dysphoria and transgender patients in general. This is definitely changing in a positive way, but a more general acceptance is going to take time. I particularly wish that gender reassignment surgeons were more supportive. They are all skilled, and most are doing a good job, but too many of them subscribe to the "there will be no hand-holding here" attitude. If a transgender surgeon doesn't want to be there emotionally for their patients, perhaps they should go into another, more neutral branch of surgery, because other than dying, the most personal thing that can happen to an individual is to change one's genitalia below the waist. Therefore, if there is any procedure in medicine that *does* require some empathy, some compassion, and—God forbid—some hand holding, it is gender reassignment surgery. I believe this will get better as more practitioners are trained.

I empathize with the difficulties that so many trans people have faced, particularly trans people of color. Sadly, many trans people have had horrid experiences as they've worked their way through the health-care system, with rejection, harassment, and mental abuse as part of the scenario. But I have also come across trans people who have negative attitudes and aggressiveness toward their doctors, which I feel is misplaced. Too often I hear complaints of physicians being difficult or "acting like a gate keeper" when all they are doing is being thorough. I believe trans people can elicit more profound change in the health-care system by working from the inside, starting a dialogue with doctors and researchers, rather than by looking for situations in which to take offense when none was meant. Mostly, though, things are changing in a positive manner.

I have also seen that on many occasions, the trans community is not as welcoming to new trans people as you might think. When I transitioned, I experienced a lot of resentment and a dismissive attitude. I think people felt threatened by me because I projected confidence, rather than seeking guidance, and they felt that I was infringing on their space. I was disappointed by this reception, and I wish that there were better, more welcoming ways to incorporate new trans people into the community, particularly older people.

I also wish that there were more of an effort being made in the medical community toward creating better procedures for trans men. Few transgender men have procedures done below the waist because there are really no good options. Currently, there is much debate in the field about what works and what doesn't work. The two bottom surgeries available to transmen are a metoidioplasty and a phalloplasty. Both of these procedures have a high rate of complications, and neither are easy for surgeons. A metoidioplasty involves incising a ligament to free up an enlarged clitoris to act like a microphallus, which, when combined with a urethral extension procedure, will (hopefully) allow the patient to urinate while standing up. However, urethral lengthening can be a particularly challenging procedure. I know some surgeons who have stopped doing metoidioplasty procedures, most likely due to the complication rate, though they don't want to say that publicly. Seemingly, this is a marketing decision, as they don't wish to be seen as any less competent of a surgeon, and there is always the option of explaining to the patient the complicated nature of the procedure.

Phalloplasty is an even more complicated and expensive surgery. For a phalloplasty, the surgeon takes a skin graft, usually from the radial forearm, and uses that material to construct a penis. This procedure is very complicated and can involve plastic surgeons, microsurgeons, and urologists. And at the end of the day, the constructed penis doesn't really work like that of a natal male. I think these patients deserve better, and I hope that going forward, we can find some improved genital surgery options for transgender men.

Overall, then, let's hope for a little bit more realism in terms of how we discuss things in transgender health. And along with that, let's hope for more professional role models for trans people. The most visible trans figures are celebrities, such as Caitlyn Jenner and Laverne Cox. Celebrity figures, whether one likes them or not, provide only one lens into the trans experience. I would like to see more profiles of public school teachers who have transitioned. Or people who are physicians, treating patients; people who are attorneys practicing law; and so forth. I realize it is not as exciting for the media to tell these stories as it is interviewing people with more exotic occupations or with a more extreme story to their life. But I want trans people to establish credibility as regular people with regular lives. This is what I'm trying to do with my life post-transition: establish recognition, credibility, and acceptance.

I also wish there was less contention within the transgender activist community. The petty bickering seems to get worse every year. The transgender community is its own worst enemy when it comes to arguing over questions of inclusion, terminology, and identity. The country is presently so polarized, that everyone has retreated to their own communities of supporters who believe the same as they do. Instead, a diversity of opinions should be accepted. Right now, in the community, one might even be attacked by those who should be allies for not towing the "party line." Personally, I am a 35-yard-line politician. Nothing is accomplished at either end of the football field; everything is accomplished between the 35-yard lines. Both sides need to try to understand the other side's viewpoint and perhaps make some compromises. People shouldn't be so overly sensitive. It is just being fair and considerate to let people voice their opinions, after which we can make an informed decision about what we want to believe.

My final wish leads right into the idea of tolerance. I wish for more trans acceptance by society, especially for those trans people living normal lives, with jobs and families of their own, outside the spotlight. I am interested in transgender medicine becoming accepted as a legitimate field of medical care. I want to see society recognize and accept the existence of gender dysphoria and transgender individuals. Going forward, I want society to take a more accepting view toward transgender health care and transgender individuals.

Overall, I am very encouraged by the direction of transgender medicine. There has been incredible progress, in terms of both potential procedures and provider acceptance, although there remains room for improvement. Nurses and medical personnel still need more education in the treatment of the transgender patient, but some medical schools and hospitals are providing that training. The next significant step forward will be moving from the challenge of trans medicine getting recognition and respect as a field to the more complicated goal of improving the available surgical techniques and refining patient selection. I also hope we can soon count on improved follow-up by doctors post-surgery and the establishment of a continuity of care for transgender patients. Surgery is not the end game for trans patients; it is only the beginning.

10 · WOULD I DO IT AGAIN?

Regrets and Mistakes I Made

IN THIS CHAPTER, I address whether the process of transitioning has left me with any regrets, and discuss whether, looking back, I would choose the same path again. I also review the mistakes I made during my transition.

REGRETS

The issue of transition regret continues to be a hot-button topic. Various surgeons appear on television, and reporters always ask them, "Do your patients have any regrets?" They, of course, never hear about any regrets, because they don't see many patients for long-term follow-up. Additionally, they are in the business of promoting their practices. When I was in the air force, we had a term for this: "geographic success." For example, I would take a third molar and transplant it into a first molar extraction site. Then, maybe two months later, somebody in the hospital or clinic would say to me, "Gee, Dr. Koch, how did that patient do with the transplant?" And I would very cavalierly reply, "I guess they're doing pretty well. They never came back with any complaints." Well, I never saw them again because the person had been transferred off the base. Thus, it was deemed a geographic success: because there was no follow-up or complaints, you got to count that surgery as a success without really knowing the result, since the patient was no longer in your geographic range. This is a common term among military doctors, since transfer happened all the time among the branches of the military. In transgender surgery, once surgery is complete and there has been some aftercare, the patient never sees the surgeon again, and if there is no follow-up and no complaints, the surgeon counts the surgery as a success, without ever knowing for sure what happened to the patient. To my knowledge, there are very few surgeons other than Dr. Meltzer who are doing active follow-ups. In my view, there should be three-year and five-year follow-ups on transgender surgical patients. How are the patients settling in to their new bodies after three years? How is their quality of life? For example, how many patients have considered or attempted suicide at the five-year point? Are they still in therapy? In pain? How are their support networks? These are questions that should be answered so that we can create an evidence-based rationale for the procedures that are being done. In my opinion, it is gaming the system when a surgeon very cavalierly says, "Well, we just don't see any regrets."

The legitimate research historically demonstrates a very low regret rate (less than 4 percent) for gender reassignment surgery patients. But I submit that this "rate of regret" is very misleading, especially for the mature individual. Certainly, I have met mature transwomen who have absolutely no regrets. But there are others who would not necessarily say that they have regrets, even if they did, because the only thing they have left is their pride. But if I phrased it a different way and asked them, "If you had a choice to do it again, would you?" they might have a different answer.

Through her website, Lynn Conway—a computer scientist at the University of Michigan—was a beacon of education and inspiration for many transwomen prior to the explosion of the transgender movement about eight years ago.[1] To her credit, in addition to transsexual success cases, she also addressed the issue of regrets.[2] Among those referenced in her article on this issue was Dr. Renée Richards, and Conway reprints a quote from a 1999 Associated Press article on Richards. I could reference more recent quotes, but I have tremendous respect for Dr. Richards:

> "It's not something for somebody in their 40s to do, someone who's had a life
> as a man. If you're 18 or 20 and never had the kind of [advantages] I had, and
> you're oriented in that direction, sure, go ahead and make right what nature
> didn't. But if you're a 45-year-old man and you're an airline pilot and you have

an ex-wife and three adolescent kids, you better get on Thorazine or Zoloft or Prozac or get locked up or do whatever it takes to keep you from being allowed to do something like this."

Dr. Conway includes other quotes from notable individuals who expressed regret or caution. Sex Change Regret is a website hosted by Walt Heyer that goes into the topic in much more depth.[3] There are numerous other websites that address transition regret as well, and there are books that address the same issue, including those from a feminist perspective. I am including the Renée Richards quote because I want all mature individuals who are considering a gender transition to be aware of the possibility of serious regret if their diagnosis is wrong and they change gender for the wrong reasons. This issue of regret should not stop mature individuals who are considering a gender transition. A successful gender transition can be accomplished at a mature age, but anyone considering such a radical procedure should be fully aware of the serious nature of their choice.

MY PERSONAL FEELINGS

So, what are my personal feelings? I do not regret undergoing gender reassignment surgery because at that point, I felt that I had no other choice. I had spent my whole life fighting the decision, and I knew that it was the choice I had to make. However, I do have other regrets. Lots of regrets.

Similar to what Dr. Richards felt and talked about in her book *No Way Renée: The Second Half of My Notorious Life*, I regret that I was gender dysphoric in the first place. It affected my life in many ways. For example, I loved athletics and was an excellent athlete. But it got to the point where I could not handle being in the men's locker room, and I simply walked away from athletic opportunities. Also, my dysphoria resulted in two less-than-ideal marriages. I never had a shouting argument with either of my two wives, and I thoroughly enjoyed the relationships I had with each woman and enjoyed being married. But I was never able to perform for both of my spouses the way I knew most men performed. I also felt cheated during all those years I had relationships with women because I was always faking it. It just didn't seem right for me to make love to a woman as a man. Consequently, I thought about being gender dysphoric every day. I was lucky, though, because it didn't make me dysfunctional, and I never once thought about committing suicide or anything like that. Sadly, gender dysphoria drives many trans people to be both dysfunctional and suicidal. This is why therapy is so important. Fortunately, I was able to avoid those issues, but gender dysphoria nonetheless greatly affected my life.

A few years ago, I was speaking to a transgender woman who had lost her entire career after transitioning and had learned that her son was going to start transitioning to become a young woman. She was ecstatic. I don't think I would share that sentiment if I were in her place. I am all for gender affirmation and finding one's place on the continuum, but the worst thing that I could wish on anybody is the gender dysphoria that accompanies being trans. There are so many challenges to being trans as compared to being born gay or straight. It is not an easy thing to figure out or experience.

My second regret about my own experience was the lack of support I had going through my transition. Part of that is the result of my ignorance. I did not realize how important therapy was. I did not realize how helpful belonging to the right support group could be. I didn't reach out to anyone. I thought, "Wait a second, I'm a pretty smart individual; I can handle this myself." As I mentioned previously, I got the physical transformation part correct, but I got the relationship part a thousand percent wrong. I was profoundly disappointed that I had no support, but I didn't know how to ask for it, either. I think this is more of a problem for the mature transitioner than for the young transitioner. Young people naturally live in larger friend groups and share more about their lives with others their age. They know how to reach out for help and support. But if you are transitioning at an older age, people have known you for a long time as your prior self. As people mature, friend groups wither, as people get more invested in their careers and families. Your coworkers and work "friends" may not be so thrilled about the changes you go through. I am a person who prided myself on being honest, but the one thing I couldn't share with anyone, and this was terrible for me, was my innermost feelings about wanting to be a woman. I presented to the world as a very masculine, successful man. How could I even think that I wanted to be a woman? I was full of shame, and I never let myself tell anyone the extent of my feelings.

Regret number three is that I wish I could have been better informed about what to expect post-surgery. I didn't have a lot of information, and the only person I can blame for that is myself. Honestly, though, I can't even fully blame myself, because the information just wasn't easily accessible. What information *did* exist at the time was principally on the Internet, and misinformation abounds online, particularly in discussions of transgender topics such as how to maintain your status in your occupation and how to have a fulfilling personal life. In reality, dating after transition is difficult, which is sad because I am so happy with and proud of my body. The sexual act itself is . . . well, you have to grow into that. There were many other issues I didn't know about, either. However, when you are older, you feel pressure to transition as soon as you can because of your age, and so I just jumped in. It is not something I am going to dwell on, but I do wish I had been better informed from the outset. Part of what I hope to achieve through this book is to have anyone, particularly mature individuals considering a gender transition, go into their transition armed with a lot more honest information than I had.

The last regret I'm going to talk about is very personal. Numerous times I was asked by my original surgeon, "Annie, don't you wish that you had done this sooner?" My stock answer was always, "Well, I wish I had done this when I was fourteen, but I am just happy to have the health and the resources to be able to do it at this stage of my life." But there is another, non–politically correct answer to this question, and it is one that deserves consideration. After seeing what has happened to other professional people I know and having experienced all the difficulties that I went through on this journey, I think, "Maybe I am actually glad that I didn't transition earlier." Think about that. I had a very productive, meaningful life, even with the burden of being gender dysphoric. I was able to compartmentalize those feelings and move ahead with my life. I was successful in my professional specialty, and I was surrounded by a lot of happy, motivated people. Certainly, things could have been worse. Currently, there is significant pressure to have a politically correct answer to everything regarding being transgender. However, the answer to the question of whether someone would have been better off doing a transition at an earlier age should be dictated on a case-by-case basis, as it is something that each person will see in a different way. Now, let's move on from the regrets.

MISTAKES AND MISCALCULATIONS

Transitioning at an advanced age is a very challenging process. Everyone who changes gender has their own unique experiences. In my case, I severely miscalculated that "it" would go away, "it" being the weight of thinking about becoming a woman every day. Now that I've transitioned, that feeling has simply been replaced with a daily review of my transition process—a rehashing of my personal experiences and individuals met along the way, combined with the ubiquitous question of whether I made a big mistake. I foolishly thought that my gender change would eradicate all these thoughts and that somehow I would start anew with a clean slate, like a do-over. No such chance; *it never goes away.* The tentacles of gender dysphoria are tenacious, and the only people who can truly appreciate this are individuals who have undergone the diagnosis.

Another miscalculation of mine was how important a good sex life was to me. I had stopped having sex with women years ago, as I felt as though I was cheating both them and myself. It just didn't seem right. However, I thought that by aligning my gender with my authentic self, my sexuality would fall into place. Fortunately, I still have tactile feelings in my neo-clitoris, but my libido is significantly reduced, and the satisfaction I feel from sexual performance is far less than I anticipated. I tried topical testosterone on my doctor's advice to increase libido, and that worked—but it was too much! At my age, I am not interested in feeling like some horny teenage boy. I was hoping to have a sexual drive that was in the normal female range. In this area, I am still a work in progress. The good news is that I feel completely re-energized and more complete than ever after having the revision and labiaplasty procedure done this past year. It has made a dramatic difference to me in terms of both self-image and sensitivity. But overall, the sexual aspect of my transition has been a disappointment.

I have also been disappointed by the response I received from LGBT health-care colleagues working in transgender medicine. After my transition, I wanted to use my medical background and my transition experience to help educate and inform these medical practitioners about the things they might be missing in the doctor-patient continuum of care, since I felt I had the unique opportunity to see it through the prisms of both a patient and an experienced health-care provider. I foolishly thought they would recognize the insight I could bring; instead, I was seen as a threat—as someone encroaching on their turf. Furthermore, the particulars of my transition experience did not necessarily match their philosophy and political agenda. So, something that I had expected to be so productive has been anything but fruitful. This has been very disappointing; medical professionals should make their practices patient based rather than use identity politics or their own personal beliefs to decide what care to provide.

In this same vein, when I was transitioning, I completely misunderstood the differences among gender surgeons. I just went with the first person I talked to about the surgery because I was so eager to have the procedure. But there are significant differences among the surgeons who perform gender reassignment surgery, not only in their surgical technique and skill, but, more importantly, in their philosophy of patient care. Please evaluate at least two surgeons before making your final decision. Your sense of abandonment can be very strong after a procedure like this, so please make certain that your surgeon is both competent and caring!

But out of everything, the biggest mistake I made was not fully informing my spouse of my intentions early on, so that she had time to get used to the idea. It would have been much easier if everything had been out in the open, and I might have had significantly more support if I had shared my need to transition with my spouse and some friends at the beginning of the process. Unfortunately, I was too embarrassed and ashamed to share my true feelings with anyone. This was a huge mistake. Support is so critical when transitioning, and the lack of support in my case can be clearly tied to my hesitancy in sharing my aspirations.

Another mistake of mine was not controlling the narrative of my transition. It took me three years before I realized the importance of getting out in front of the story of my transition—that is, explaining what was happening and why. Once I decided on the story to tell people, it made my life easier both socially and with my business connections. You must be proactive in coming up with your own story that explains what you're doing and why. When you are transitioning at an advanced age, you cannot sit back and wait for people to realize on their own what is happening. Nor can you expect any help if you don't ask for it. It is absolutely imperative that you control the narrative right out of the gate and make sure that your trusted friends and family, once they are comfortable with the knowledge, can retell the story *you* want them to tell.

POSITIVE DEVELOPMENTS

I did experience a number of positive developments during and after transitioning. I absolutely love my body, and I am pleased with my overall

FIGURE 26. Two-year GRS anniversary, March 25, 2015 (65+ years old)
This picture was taken in Hawaii at my friend's condominium on the second-year anniversary of my GRS procedure. I am very comfortable with both my appearance and my physicality. I try to stay in shape physically, and I hope that anyone who transitions at a mature age does likewise. I am over sixty-five in this picture.

appearance. I think I look very age appropriate and non-artificial. I am also pleased with the final outcome of the work my surgeons performed. I think their combined efforts make me look younger than my chronological age. Being this age, I am pleased that I have good health and that I am active, but for me, having the correct genitalia and a functioning vagina is also very important. In my mind, it completes me as a woman. Of course, this is just *my* opinion and *my situation* that I'm talking about. Other situations may vary, and everyone considering a transition should make sure they pursue a course of action that validates their own existence.

I am also pleased at how I have been able to assimilate into regular society in my day-to-day life. As previously mentioned, I didn't realize how traditional I am as an individual until I transitioned and started examining my life. I accept and support the notion of a gender continuum in general, but I have come to realize that I am most comfortable in the binary world. Certainly, being a transsexual woman is part of me, but it does not define me. I am Anne Koch. I hope that people see Anne as an energetic person who has had a lot of life experience. As someone said to me, "You've got moxie!" I hope so—if I do, it was well earned. My assimilation has been far more seamless than I ever could have imagined, and I consider myself lucky that I have been able to live the way I do. The journey has not been easy.

Finally, I am pleased that I have been able to start working in my dental specialty again, and I have recently been welcomed back with open arms. I speak at many dental conferences, including those in my specialty. When I present, I talk about the different techniques I have created, such as the use of bioceramics in endodontics, and I talk about transgender issues in dentistry. In March 2017, I found myself presenting as the keynote speaker at the annual conference of the American Dental Education Association, the world's largest dental education conference. I never could have imagined this when I started my transition—never! The best thing that I can do for other professional trans women is to re-establish myself in my profession. I am back to writing articles, giving lectures, and developing techniques and products. I am engaged again with colleagues. People are discovering that Anne Koch is a much more entertaining lecturer than Ken Koch ever was. In fact, my schedule is heavily booked. I am so thankful for the attention, and I consider myself very fortunate. But I have also worked damn hard to get to this point.

As a side note to what I've said about my career comeback, I am so lucky to have had a life in which I was productive and functional as a man, and to

FIGURE 27. Dr. Anne Koch lecturing, University of Illinois, Chicago School of Dental Medicine, 2018

"The Annie Show" at the University of Illinois at Chicago, College of Dentistry. What a wonderful group of students, residents, and faculty members. I thoroughly enjoyed my two days with them. I try to get around to as many dental and medical schools as possible. So much about understanding transition is an education issue.

now be approaching that same level of success as a woman. However, I think misogyny in general medicine, dental medicine, and veterinary medicine is worse now than it was in 1975. And part of the reason is that these days, there are so many male doctors in schools or in private practice as senior partners who come from cultures where misogyny is not only tolerated but promoted. I have been a victim of this myself, and I am more than willing to back up my female colleagues in supporting women's rights. I am a feminist, and the more transwomen there are in professional roles, the more visible we will be and the better able we will be to advocate for all women.

THE MILLION-DOLLAR QUESTION

Now that I've discussed my regrets and mistakes, as well as some of the positive developments after my transition, it is worth noting that as I write this book, it has been six years since I first went to see Dr. Spiegel for a consultation. Enough time has passed that I can look back at my transition retrospectively, and I do have some meaningful observations.

The million-dollar question is, Would I do it again? At this point, you probably think the answer is a firm yes or no. Truthfully, I do not have a definitive answer for you—there is no easy answer—but I can tell you what my thinking is. I would do it again if the only consideration were my personal physical transformation. I love the way I look, and I feel as though I am finally the person I felt like I was inside my whole life. However, I am a social person, and even though I have a lot of friends and am known and accepted by the community at large, I'm still very lonely. I would love to meet somebody and fall in love. That type of relationship would be amazing to find now, and it doesn't even matter to me if it's with a man or a woman, cis or trans. My preference would be to be with a woman, but I just want to find another human being who loves me for who I am, and whom I can love in return. I want to find someone I can support and care for. I have done many things in my life, and thankfully, most were done successfully. However, I want to be able to share my experience with a life partner and help them in their career. I also realize that having children can be wonderful, and I missed out on that when I was Ken. Even at this point in my life, I am looking for a family.

One time I was hitting tennis balls against a wall on Easter morning in Hawaii. An older Asian gentleman passed by, and he said, "Excuse me, madam, but I have been watching you hit balls. You have great strokes. Do you play competitively?" I said I did. We started chatting, and he mentioned that he was a retired tennis pro who worked on the East End of Long Island in the Hamptons. He then said to me, "I have a question. It's Easter morning. How come you are not with your family?" I looked at him and simply said, "I have no family," and went back to hitting tennis balls against the wall.

The one thing that doesn't sit right with me post-transition is that I wish I had more of a family. I hate the loneliness. If over the course of the next few years, by the time I am seventy years old, I do not find somebody to love, the answer to the question, Would I do it again? might be no. However, if I can find a way to have a relationship and have that give meaning to the last 20 percent of my life, then I would absolutely transition again. But right now, the change in my life has been so difficult to navigate, and I have lost so much, that sometimes I waver. I never expected to find myself alone at this point in my life, and the loneliness can be terrible. Fortunately, I am not prone to depression, but I can well imagine how this type of loneliness can lead to pronounced depression. And depression is a serious issue for many trans people, as it contributes to a high attempted-suicide rate: 41 percent of trans people have attempted suicide at one time or another.

These days, I spend a lot of time lecturing at medical and dental schools, and during my visits, I meet many different individuals. Perhaps there is an open-minded faculty member at one of these places who is at a certain point in their career and who finds me attractive and is willing to accept my trans status. In fact, perhaps they see it as an enhancement. Realistically, I think the chance of this happening is very slight, but it makes a great fantasy. And who knows? By putting my desire out there, maybe I'm willing the universe to make it happen.

CONCLUSION

At the end of the day, then, there are two big questions post-transition. In terms of whether someone has regrets, when people are pressed, even those who have been devastated by transitioning at a mature age say they do not have any regrets, because if nothing else, we all have our pride. But the question of whether someone would do it again is much more introspective and requires deliberation. That is why, for me, the honest answer is, "I don't know." But I have given you my parameters. I love how I look and feel, but I need to be in a relationship in order to make this entire process seem like a worthwhile and wise decision. This is only *my* opinion. Yours may be very different, but I wish that whatever decision you make, it is a truthful one. That is what this book is about; it is meant to help you transition in a way that is safe and productive, and help you make an informed, successful transition as a mature individual.

11 · EPILOGUE

THE FIRST THREE years following my transition were very difficult. I felt estranged from my profession, confused in my social context, and abandoned in my continuity of care as a transgender patient. The exception to this downward spiral occurred on December 26, 2014.

During the 2014 Christmas holidays, my cousin visited me, and the day after Christmas, we went to visit one of Dr. Spiegel's patients, who had had facial feminization surgery right before Christmas. I visited this person in the same Boston hotel where I had stayed during my own surgery, and my cousin went with me to keep me company. She remained in the hotel lobby while I visited with this person. When I was done, my cousin and I went for a cup of coffee at my favorite coffee shop in the North End of Boston. I had just been speaking to my cousin about how bad I felt that I had lost contact with my best friend from dental school, John Ward. We were incredibly good friends back then; we actually spent one summer living on a boat in Montauk, fishing. I had even sent John a Christmas card and called his office in Texas to see if I could find him. They told me that he had sold his practice. I really thought that I was never going to see him again.

John grew up in Charlestown, Massachusetts, which borders the North End of Boston, and as I was sitting there with my cousin, I looked across the café. I saw this person sitting there and realized I was looking at John Ward. I knew he had a bunch of brothers, and he looked like he was sitting with one of them. I also remembered that he sometimes visited his mother during the holidays. I mentioned all of this to my cousin, and I finally got up and walked over to the table where John and his brother were sitting. I said,

"Excuse me, sir, but are you Dr. John V. Ward Jr.?" I knew he would respond to me, because most people don't refer to him that way in Boston. He said he was, and looked at me quizzically. I said, "Well, you know me."

He said, "I do?" Then he added, "I don't know, but I think I . . ."

I said, "No, you do. Please come with me." He got up and actually came with me. We stopped halfway across the coffee shop floor, and he was looking at me totally confused. I repeated, "You know me!"

He replied, "Really?"

I said, "Yeah." He was looking at me, trying to figure out the accent, thinking, Who is this person? Then I used an odd expression that only the two of us used fishing: "John, fluke at Shagwong."

He said, "What?"

I repeated, "Fluke, Shagwong."

He pointed at me hesitantly and said, "Ken?"

I replied, "Was!" He finally realized who I was, and we hugged and jumped up and down. It was like a scene from a Hollywood movie.

Later on, my cousin said, "When you connected, everyone in the coffee shop was so happy looking at the two of you." It was so amazing to find him again after all that time. My friend John is a typical garrulous Boston Irishman, but he was tongue-tied. He was so stunned at running into me this way. We talked for a bit, just a few minutes, and then he had to leave with his brother. But he later made contact three separate times to talk and validate the incredible fact that his good friend Ken Koch was now a woman. I also think he came back because he just couldn't believe that we had connected so randomly after all these years. This was such an amazing experience for me. That chance encounter with my best friend was a great send-off to 2014.

In 2015, things were still going a bit sideways, but I was making a new life for myself on Cape Cod. Eventually, as I mentioned before, I had to sell the home in Florida that I had owned with my wife. However, as part of the divorce settlement, we were able to get a beautiful thirty-seventh floor ocean-side condominium in Hawaii for Akiko. I was genuinely pleased that it was such a nice place. I felt good that she was being taken care of in such a positive way, and our relationship was getting better; overall, 2015 was off to a pretty good start. That summer, Akiko joined me on Cape Cod after I visited her in Hawaii. We were starting to get to know each other as friends again, and it was fun.

The next really big turning point for me came that summer when I received an email from the alumni office of the University of Pennsylvania Dental School. It said, "We discovered that you no longer live in West Palm Beach and that you have changed your name." Obviously, they knew, so I called the alumni office. I spoke to a woman who was completely understanding of the situation. She was wonderful, and the next day I received the most heartfelt, humanistic email that I have ever received in my life. It was from my former mentor, Dr. Syngcuk Kim. I couldn't believe that he had sent me such an incredible email. Dr. Kim is a world-renowned endodontic microsurgeon, and although he had been my mentor, I was stunned that he had taken the time to write such a meaningful email. One thing led to another, and I was invited to go down to the University of Pennsylvania School of Dental Medicine for an unofficial Anne Koch Day. It was amazing—all these people welcomed me back. Penn Dental School has a large LGBTQ group named AMALGAM, and we had dinner together. I took a picture of the group, which is still on my fireplace mantle. It was amazing to have such support when I was still in the middle of rebuilding my life.

When I left after the two days, I gave a little speech and started to cry. I couldn't believe how kind everyone had been to me. In fact, in many aspects, Penn has become my family. Over the course of the next few months, I was treated so wonderfully that I stepped up and made a very significant donation to the dental school, which ultimately culminated in 2017 with the dedication of the Anne L. Koch room. It's a large lecture and seminar room named A Place to Call Our Own. It is a room that was "gifted in recognition of LGBT students, residents, faculty and staff."

During the summer of 2015, I also entered the New England Women's Senior Tennis Championship. This was a big deal for me because I had been starting to enjoy my life as a woman, and I was finally able to enjoy athletics again.

In November, right before Thanksgiving, Akiko visited from Hawaii again. She went with me to Cornell University, so I could present at IvyQ, the largest pan–Ivy League LGBTQ conference, for a second time. Afterward, we watched Cornell's hockey team and had a fun dinner in Ithaca. This seemed to be a harbinger of good things, as Thanksgiving was much better, and Christmas was starting to become enjoyable again. On New Year's Eve, there was another significant moment. Akiko and I were sitting in a very nice restaurant in Chatham when I made a decision. On New Year's Eve in Japan, it

FIGURE 28. Dr. Anne L. Koch room, University of Pennsylvania, 2017
The Anne L. Koch room at the University of Pennsylvania School of Dental Medicine.
This room has been gifted in recognition of LGBT students, residents, faculty, and
staff. I am so honored to have been able to do this.

is a Buddhist ritual to ring bells numerous times. I said to Akiko, "Did you
hear those bells?"

She said, "No. I didn't hear anything."

I said, "I'm just kidding, there are no bells. I heard them in my mind. Those
bells were ringing because time has run out." I had just decided that I no longer wanted to waste any effort on my old friends who still would not speak
to me and would not even respond to an email. I decided then that I was not
going to reach out any longer. Instead, I decided to step up, get my energy
back, and move forward with my life without them. This was a momentous
decision. I realized that from that point forward, I had to take control of my
life. I had sat around for a few years, feeling sorry for myself. I was lost and
confused, and I kept hoping that someone would step up and help me or
show me the way. Nobody helped me, either personally or professionally.
People just wanted money. I finally realized that with what had happened at
Penn, playing in the women's tennis tournament, and presenting at IvyQ, this
was all about me controlling the message. I was saying to the world that I was
Anne Koch, and I belonged. This really changed my world. I had finally

stopped waiting for the acceptance and approval of other people and started accepting myself.

PROFESSIONAL MILESTONES

Going into 2016, things started to move for me. I organized a transgender medicine conference with Lisa McBride, someone I had met the previous year at the Building the Next Generation of Academic Physicians (BNGAP) conference in New York City. We met after a lecture when she identified herself as the diversity officer for the Philadelphia College of Osteopathic Medicine. I asked her if she had ever thought about putting together a transgender medicine conference, and that was the beginning of a marvelous relationship. Eventually, we ended up staging the transgender medicine conference in March 2016 at the Philadelphia College of Osteopathic Medicine. It was a watershed event in many ways. The conference brought researchers and doctors together, and everyone was treating trans medicine as a legitimate field of study. Additionally, it was nice to see transgender medicine in an academic spotlight in real life, rather than on the Internet. I was very pleased to be involved with the conference, both behind the scenes and as a presenter.

Following the conference, I was the featured speaker at the LGBT Workforce Conference at Weill Cornell Medical College. There were 238 physicians and some medical students in attendance. I showed pictures of my transition during my lecture and addressed many different topics. It was a wonderful session, and I got a standing ovation. Afterward, I received many invitations to speak at medical schools or at specific conferences. Professionally, life was starting to go in the direction that I had hoped it would.

As I moved into 2017, my life had become totally different from how it was when I started my transition. I found myself presenting all over the country, both in my dental specialty and at trans medical conferences. I have been a keynote speaker at many medical schools and conferences. For example, at Rutgers University, I presented to over 350 people. My dream for myself post-transition has always been to be accepted as a stylish and classy professional woman, and it is finally coming true.

In March 2017, along with political commentators Hilary Rosen and Ana Navarro, I had the opportunity to be a keynote speaker at the largest dental education conference in the world, that of the ADEA (American Dental Education Association). In addition to being one of the featured keynote speakers, I gave a ninety-minute presentation called "Treating the Transgender Dental Patient." Both my keynote address and my panel went very well, and Dr. Richard Valachovic, chairperson of the ADEA, wrote a very nice column afterward about my participation:

DIVERSITY AND INCLUSION

Like many of our previous plenary speakers, Jemison, Navarro, and Rosen had star power. No doubt about it. But arguably, the brightest light at this year's Annual Session was supplied by Anne Koch, D.M.D.—an endodontist, entrepreneur, and faculty colleague of mine from our time together at the Harvard School of Dental Medicine—who spoke about the needs of transgender patients and her own experience transitioning. She addressed a packed audience at a morning seminar that officially ended at noon, but unofficially continued to almost 3:00 P.M., while Anne answered questions and talked one-on-one with attendees. A few hours later, she headlined our new Sunday evening plenary, "In the Mix" Series: Inclusion, Excellence, and Dental Education—a time for members to actively network with one another while exploring the many faces of diversity and inclusion.

I don't remember the last time we had a dental educator as a plenary speaker, but having one of our own speak to these particular issues was extremely powerful. If you've already met Anne, you know she has an open and engaging personality. She's also a dynamic presenter. You could hear a pin drop during her remarks, and when the discussion portion of the plenary began, everyone participated. Without a doubt, this new event on diversity and inclusion was a huge hit and highlight of the Annual Session for many. Anne's assessment? She told me, "I felt like I belonged at this meeting for the first time."

Likewise, in April 2017, I had the opportunity to be a keynote speaker at Dentaltown's annual Townie Meeting held in Las Vegas. It was tremendous fun, and I did follow-up podcasts for Dentaltown as well. But after the Dentaltown meeting, I went to New Orleans and presented at my specialty meeting, the American Association of Endodontists. This was a big deal for me. Naturally, I had presented many times at this meeting over the course of my career, but this was my first time presenting as Dr. Anne Koch. Furthermore, in addition to presenting on a technique that I had co-developed—using bioceramic technology in endodontics—I gave a presentation called "Treating the Transgender Endodontic Patient." I never felt prouder to be an endodontist than when I gave that presentation. Both presentations went well, and most of the questionnaires from the trans presentation were positive. I am proud to call those people my colleagues. However, some comments were written on the feedback forms that were not only not positive but also not constructively critical. Instead, they were just insulting and mean. That just proves that there is more work to be done in the field around educating medical professionals about transgender medicine and transgender patients, and I am ready to address that need. It galvanizes my commitment.

UP TO THE PRESENT

While I achieved numerous milestones in my professional life in 2017, everything was not perfect. As previously mentioned, my physical anatomy still wasn't quite what I wanted it to be. I wanted to have genitalia that looked as natural as possible, and the results of my initial surgery were not satisfactory. So I made an appointment for a labiaplasty/surgical revision with Dr. Toby Meltzer in Scottsdale. I had the revision surgery done in November 2017, and this time, the results, along with the entire patient experience, far exceeded my expectations and showed me what was really possible in the way of continuity of care.

I am finally settling into my new life. Friends continually tell me how happy I look. I have heard this so many times that I think it is a direct result of my being very comfortable in my own skin. I am finally starting to live as my true self, and a large part of this is due to my physical anatomy. Dr. Meltzer's procedure gave me what I'd been hoping for five years ago. I have always been very pleased with Dr. Spiegel's results on my face, and now I feel the same way about my genitalia. It has made a huge difference in my contentment; I am finally happy.

I have continued to rebuild my professional career by speaking at numerous dental conferences, and I am always gratified by the invitations and the response to my talks. I am most happy when presenting and answering questions. I will answer any question directly and honestly, as I believe the acceptance of transgender individuals is an education issue, and I realize most people never get the chance to ask the questions they are most curious about.

I also made the recent decision to endow two fellowship programs. At the Philadelphia College of Osteopathic Medicine, I am endowing a five-year webinar and lecture series on transgender health care; and at the Harvard School of Dental Medicine, I am sponsoring a five-year program on diversity and inclusion, including women's issues. I was also happy to re-establish my faculty status at Harvard.

Another interesting development has been my emergence as a mentor for many professional women in both medicine and dentistry. In fact, I have created a new presentation, "The Entrepreneurial Woman Doctor," in which I talk about how to protect intellectual property, how best to market oneself, and how to put together a start-up company. The response to this presentation has been terrific, and I feel as though I have hit my stride by fronting for women's issues in both medicine and business.

FINAL THOUGHTS

As I review the past six years and contemplate how my personal transition has evolved, I realize that a gender transition is not only unique to each individual but remains a very fluid process, continuing to evolve as one goes on in their new life. I have come through the medical part successfully, but even six years in, I am still discovering new insights, and as a mature individual, I have a lot of previous life to which to compare these new experiences.

Certainly, people can see the difference in me. Part of that difference is that I have enormous energy now. It's ironic, but doing this transition later in life has given me an energy level that I never thought I would have at this point in my life. I am sixty-eight years old, and I am still trying to rock it. That's a message for all women!

On just about every day of my life up until March 25, 2013, at some point I thought about being a woman. But after having my surgical procedures, that feeling went away. There are a lot of difficulties associated with transitioning, but one of the positives is that my feeling of wishing, hoping, longing to be a member of the opposite sex has left, and I am thankful for that. However, although my desire to become a woman went away, it has been replaced by the constant worry that I've made a mistake. Maybe this will go away soon as well, but I think it's probably going to be with me for the rest of my life. Transition is just not easy, especially when you do it as a mature adult. You simply cannot erase sixty-three years of a life. Even if it isn't a perfect life, it's still your own. And mine wasn't a bad life at all. It wasn't like I was dysfunctional or suicidal; I was very functional, very successful. But now I have a different persona, a different life. In some ways, my life now is nothing like it was before. But I was a happy person as Ken. In fact, an ex–business associate of mine, who was extremely stunned when I told him about my plans to transition, said, "I can't believe it. If I had to name the two or three happiest people I have ever met in my life, I would say you're one of them. How can you possibly think about doing this?" Indeed. Sometimes I wonder myself. Mostly, though, I'm happy as Annie and at peace with my decision.

I also find that in many instances, I still think like Ken—like a man. Sometimes I have to make an effort to think like a woman. As I mentioned earlier, I know that I will never be exactly like a natal woman, but I am trying to get as close to that as I can. By transitioning at such an advanced age, it makes sense to me that I am never going to be able to eradicate everything from my old life. Furthermore, I don't mind that. I have reached a specific gravity that is very comfortable to me. Plus, I have the unique perspective of having been successful as a man in my specialty and working as a successful professional woman in the same specialty. It just seems logical that at times I would have to make a little bit of an effort to respond or act like a cisgender woman would. I have finally reached the point where I don't turn around if someone says, "Excuse me, sir." That's a key milestone for transwomen. But if someone says, "Ken," I still feel a little bit of acknowledgment of that name on my side.

ANNIE/KEN, KEN/ANNIE

I am only now getting to the point where I can throw out trophies and awards that I had won or been given as Ken. Saying goodbye to him is still very painful. It's not like I hated Ken. I thought Ken was in many ways a terrific person. So, the enormity of doing away with him, basically killing Ken, is not an easy thing with which to live. I think that many people who transition feel the same way. People sometimes make it seem like when you transition, you'll be going up a golden staircase into a beautiful life full of contentment. Nonsense. It's not easy to transition and change your whole way of thinking and living, even if you really want it, and it is particularly hard if you're transitioning at a mature age. In many ways, I remain the same person as Ken. I still like watching Stanley Cup hockey on television. I still dislike soccer. But it is different now, too. I see Ken as my brother and, in many ways, my twin brother. I am sure that this is quite common among transsexual women, and I am disappointed that more people don't ask me how I see my former self. I know that many trans people will not share information about their prior lives, and apparently some people find it emotionally damaging to even discuss it. I understand that; more importantly, I respect that. But for me, the situation is quite different. I am very proud of my former life. In fact, I am very transparent about my former identity, and I even had a psychiatrist at a medical school where I was lecturing tell me that they were concerned with my "openness." I honestly have no problem being transparent. It doesn't bother me. The truth is, I enjoy talking about my prior life, but I don't think that is a very common trait among trans people. In the end, though, I have learned to enjoy having the capacity to see life through two lenses: that of a mature, successful woman and that of a mature, successful man. That's just who I am now.

THE HANGOVER—IT'S NOT JUST A MOVIE

I truly feel as if I have come through the valley of death. Those first few years were awful. Having survived that experience, there is nothing that can make me either fearful or overly anxious anymore. Nothing scares me—it's as simple as that. Honestly, my gender transition brought me far more pain than joy during the first five years. I imagine this could be different for other people. It might have even been different for me if I'd been significantly dysfunctional as a man, but as I've noted, I was very functional as a man. In this sixth year, the joyous part of being a woman is now just beginning. My professional life has become fulfilling again. I'm enjoying athletics for the first time in a long while, and many of my social activities and relationships have also come back. But I do miss the personal aspect of having a partner—someone you can really love and who loves and cares about you.

When reading articles about gender transition, I often come across the term "hangover." This is a term used within transgender communities, although it is also sometimes used in an anti-trans manner. What I am referring to when I use this term is that there is a fairly natural, letdown in one's expectations after pushing so hard for a number of years to reach the goal of

FIGURE 29. My nephew and his son, Christmas 2015

With my nephew and his son at Christmastime. It took some time, but I am so pleased and thankful to have my extended family relationships back. One must give this time, because a transition affects so many people.

a surgical transition. It is a completely exhausting experience: physically, emotionally, and financially. Consequently, some individuals become depressed and pessimistic when things don't magically become perfect right after their transition. There is merit in acknowledging this period, because it requires effort to push through it. The hangover can occur anytime from two to five years post-surgery, and its effect varies on a case-by-case basis. In addition to one's own convictions and fortitude, having a network of support is critical in moving forward in a positive way. Therapy is strongly advised in those instances where the hangover becomes problematic.

No one ever talks about their negative feelings in relation to their transition. Because of identity politics, nobody feels as if they can say, "This experience is not working out the way I thought it would. I'm not as happy as I thought I would be. This is a lot more difficult than I ever imagined." But the feelings come through nonetheless. I feel it myself some days, and I see it in some of my medical and dental colleagues who have transitioned. Their lives have become so messy, and they seem unhappy. A number of them have gone through relationships that have been abusive. Some have had no relationships. Some still have physiological issues. At the end of the day, I hope that everyone can find some happiness, but it's not as easy as just changing body parts.

I don't think I'm any happier as a woman. If I can just be as happy as a woman as I was as Ken, that works for me. But what I am discovering is that my level of contentment seems higher. Life will go on, and I will go on. That's how I feel. I am very pleased that I have been rejuvenated, and I am still reconfirming in my mind every day that this is what was meant to be. This transition meant so much to me, and it is sad that other people in my life don't see it that way. The people in transgender medicine see me as a check and a record number, and at the end of the day, some of my friends still see it as bad judgment. And others still see it as being if not frivolous then totally selfish. As my ex-spouse said to me at one point, "The only person you've ever loved is yourself." That is not true. I hope someday she realizes how much I loved her and how much I could still love her. But this type of huge life change is not an easy thing to process—for anyone.

I want to conclude my story on a positive note because, although difficult, a gender change can be accomplished successfully at a mature age.

In July 2017, Smithtown Central High School Class of 1967 celebrated its fiftieth high school reunion. I attended this event for two evenings, and it was

FIGURE 30. Football teammates, Smithtown Central High School 50th Reunion, Long Island, NY, July 2017

This is a wonderful picture of me with two former high school football teammates at our fiftieth reunion. It was two of the greatest days in my life, and I will be forever thankful for having such good, loyal friends. I cannot think of any better way to end this book than my fiftieth high school reunion.

one of the greatest experiences of my life. We had an amazing turnout, and it was fun to reconnect with my classmates. Most of them seemed to know about my change and had seen pictures. I very much appreciated some of my female classmates who made the effort to inform others in my class before the reunion. Things went very smoothly.

I was thrilled to be received in such an accepting manner. My classmates were incredible. I also had a great time speaking with my former football teammates, and the co-captain of the team even asked me to dance. His only comment was, "Annie, you can't lead." I cannot fully express how much this reunion meant to me and how grateful I was for the welcome reception I was given by my classmates. I had been confident that they would be okay with my transition, because I had already been in touch with many of my friends from high school, but their response and love exceeded my wildest expectations. It is something that I will never forget. I loved high school, and I truly enjoyed my classmates; now, I love them even more. A former football teammate said to me, "You'll always be our quarterback and our leader." That meant so much to me. You can change the exterior, but you're still the same person on the inside. I knew my classmates would have my back, but I never could have imagined just how loving they would be. Thank you, Smithtown Central High School Class of 1967!

As I weaved my way through writing this book, it gave me the opportunity to examine various aspects of my transition through a different prism. It is never easy to condense multiple experiences and impressions, but I am going to list ten final thoughts from my personal journey. I hope you've learned something about me as a person, but more important, I hope I've provided a bit more knowledge around what a gender transition is like and helped give everyone who may be thinking about transitioning a blueprint of things to consider.

1. Doing a gender transition at a mature age was not what I had expected. It was far more difficult than anticipated, in part due to the significant amount of misinformation that I encountered. I could not believe the amount of bullshit I heard about what to expect, from both medical providers and people in their own political ghettos on the Internet. This confusion of viewpoints does a disservice to anyone attempting a transition. The truth needs to be told, both the positive aspects and the negative.

2. I was surprised that transgender medicine had not evolved as much as I had imagined it had. Poor patient selection, lack of real follow-up post-surgery, and the absence of continuity of care were all problems that I quickly recognized and experienced. The good news is that these challenges are currently being addressed by the medical community, and I expect to see continued improvement in these areas.

3. I was so fortunate to have connected with both Dr. Jeffrey Spiegel and Dr. Toby Meltzer. These gentlemen absolutely represent competent and caring surgeons. They changed my life, and I will be forever grateful.

4. There are too many people gaming the system. This applies to patients and providers alike. I wholeheartedly believe that there is legitimacy in a diagnosis of gender dysphoria, but my concern is that too many people are profiting from the system in one way or another and that the legitimacy of the diagnosis is being diluted.

5. For a mature transitioner, the best facial plastic surgery procedure to have is a neck lift. It totally changes your profile and makes you look much younger. My second recommendation is a lip lift.

6. Clinical depression post-surgery is very real and can be a significant issue for many GRS patients. It is particularly troublesome for young patients but can be an issue for patients of any age. Even cardiac surgery patients have a reported 50 percent incidence of post-op depression. Recognize it, understand that it is natural, and don't hesitate to seek professional help.

7. Mature individuals may take significant time—up to four to five years in some cases—to adjust to their new bodies and new genders. Please allow ample time for your friends and family to come around. It took some serious time for my family to fully comprehend my decision, and it took friends even longer. Yes, I lost some friends in the process, but many have returned. Be patient. A gender transition affects people in different ways.

8. Along those lines, you must control the dialogue of your gender transition from the start. Don't go in expecting a lot of help. In many ways, you are on your own, but you can at least set out your expectations for your friends and family so that they are prepared beforehand with the story that you want them to tell. At the end of the day, it is you who must determine the course of the rest of your life, so it is better to start out with the narrative that you want promulgated.

9. Don't fall prey to transition hangover. It happens to many people, and you need to stay confident in your choice and drive through this period. If the regret or uncertainty becomes overwhelming, seek professional help. There are many therapists and hospitals that can help you navigate this difficult and stressful period.

10. Finally, no one is disposable. I am committed to bringing sensibility, credibility, and acceptability to the issue of gender dysphoria. It is my sincere hope that this book will help people thinking about a transition determine the right course of action for themselves and help demystify the process a bit.

ACKNOWLEDGMENTS

First, I want to acknowledge all the women working in the offices of gender reassignment surgeons. Whether they are nurses, physician assistants, or staff personnel, these women offer the transgender patient support, comfort, and encouragement. They are the bridge between the surgeon and your new life. Simply put, the task of transitioning could not be accomplished without their contribution and compassion. Ladies, thank you for your humanity!

I also must acknowledge my editor, Kimberly Guinta, without whom this book would not have been possible. Throughout the process, Kim offered her guidance, advice, and encouragement. She was fully engaged and somehow managed to get me to share my entire story. This is what great editors do: they get the complete story out of you! Among other things, Kim made me realize that a gender transition profoundly affects everyone, not just the person undergoing the transition. But, more importantly, she made me evaluate my own transition in ways that no one heretofore had even remotely suggested. For this, I am deeply appreciative.—ALK

NOTES

CHAPTER 9   REALITY, MYTHS, AND THE FUTURE OF TRANSGENDER HEALTH CARE

1. Hannes Sigurjónsson, Johan Rinder, Caroline Möllermark, Filip Farnebo, and T. Kallie Lundgren, "Male to Female Gender Reassignment Surgery: Surgical Outcomes of Consecutive Patients during 14 Years," *JPRAS Open*, October 23, 2015.
2. Paulette Cutruzzula Dreher, Daniel Edwards, Shaun Hager, Margeaux Dennis, Andie Belkoff, Jamie Mora, Susan Tarry, and Kathy L. Rumer, "Complications of the Neovagina in Male-to-Female Transgender Surgery: A Systematic Review and Meta-analysis with Discussion of Management," *Clinical Anatomy* 31, no. 2 (March 2018): 191–199.
3. Thomas W. Gaither, Mohannad A. Awad, E. Charles Osterberg, Gregory P. Murphy, Angelita Romero, Marci L. Bowers, and Benjamin N. Breyer, "Postoperative Complications Following Primary Penile Inversion Vaginoplasty among 330 Male-to-Female Transgender Patients," *Journal of Urology* 199, no. 3 (March 2018): 760–765.
4. Ebba K. Lindquist, Hannes Sigurjónsson, Caroline Möllermark, Johan Rinder, Filip Farnebo, and T. Kallie Lundgren, "Quality of Life Improves Early after Gender Reassignment Surgery in Transgender Women," *European Journal of Plastic Surgery* 40, no. 3 (2017): 22326.
5. Cecilia Dhejne, Paul Lichtenstein, Marcus Boman, Anna L. V. Johansson, Niklas Långström, and Mikael Landén, "Long-Term Follow-Up of Transsexual Persons Undergoing Sex Reassignment Surgery: Cohort Study in Sweden," *PLoS One* 6, no. 2 (February 2011): e16885.
6. Hannes Sigurjónsson, "Outcome and Refinements of Gender Confirmation Surgery" (PhD diss., Karolinska Institutet, Sweden, December 16, 2016).
7. Sidhbh Gallagher, "What Is Pelvic Floor Physical Therapy?" University of Indiana Gender Confirmation, https://universitygenderaffirmationsurgery.com 2017.
8. Sigurjónsson et al., "Male to Female Gender Reassignment Surgery."
9. Sara Solovitch, "When Kids Come in Saying They Are Transgender (or No Gender), These Doctors Try to Help," *Washington Post*, January 21, 2018.
10. Stephen B. Levine, "Ethical Concerns about Emerging Treatment Paradigms for Gender Dysphoria," *Journal of Sex and Marital Therapy* 44, no. 1 (2018).
11. Janet Albrechtsen, "First Cut Is the Deepest but Reversal Also Traumatic for Trans Community," *Australian*, October 28, 2017.
12. Kellan E. Baker, "The Future of Transgender Coverage," *New England Journal of Medicine*, April 5, 2017, http://www.nejm.org/doi/10.1056/NEJMp1702427.

13. Alessandra Potenza, "Gender Confirmation Surgery Improves Transgender People's Lives Research Confirms, March 22, 2018, www.theverge.com/2018/3/22/17144814 /gender-confirmation-surgery-quality-of-life-transgender-people-dysphoria.

CHAPTER 10   WOULD I DO IT AGAIN?

1. See Lynn's website at http://ai.eecs.umich.edu/people/conway/conway.html.
2. See http://ai.eecs.umich.edu/people/conway/TS/Warning.html.
3. See www.sexchangeregret.com.

INDEX

academic abilities of Koch, 4, 5, 7
Adam's apple, 50, 60
adolescence: gender dysphoria in, 161;
    of Koch, 3–5
aesthetic outcome: in breast augmentation,
    79, 87, 99; in facial feminization surgery,
    60; in gender reassignment surgery, 82,
    89–90, 91, 92, 159, 176
Affordable Care Act, 137, 162
age in transition process, 123–124, 133–134;
    and breast augmentation, 81, 85, 87, 88; and
    dating, 142–144; and difficulties experi-
    enced, 187–188, 193; and ethical issues, 160,
    161; and facial feminization surgery, 59, 60,
    124, 194; and gender reassignment surgery,
    92, 93, 94, 95, 98, 107, 124, 161, 164–165, 172;
    and hormone therapy, 85, 120, 134–135; and
    life goals, 128; and loneliness, 138–142;
    and mistakes, 172–173, 174; and mortality
    sense, 127; and personal relationships,
    118–119, 138–144; and regrets, 172; and
    sexual satisfaction, 144–146; and support
    system, 171; and therapy, 101–102, 105, 106,
    107, 108, 110, 113, 115, 116
Air Force service of Koch: in Japan, 20–27,
    28–30; in Korea, 28, 29f; in New Jersey,
    30–31
AMALGAM group, 182
American Association of Endodontists,
    55, 185
American Dental Education Association,
    176, 185
Anderson, Erica, 161
athletic abilities of Koch, 4, 148–149, 150f,
    170; in high school, 5–12, 192f, 193; and
    locker room use, 13, 148–149, 170; at
    Rutgers, 13, 14, 15f

Baker, Kellan E., 162
Barton's bandage, 45, 58

baseball, Koch playing, 4, 12, 14, 15f
basketball, Koch playing, 8f
bathrooms, public, 39, 129
Biber, Stanley, 27
blepharoplasty, 43–44, 46, 50
body odor changes, 135
Boston Medical Center: Center for
    Transgender Medicine and Surgery at,
    45, 53, 92, 93; facial feminization surgery
    at, 44–45
breast augmentation surgery, 78–81, 85–89;
    age at time of, 81, 85, 87, 88; consultation
    for, 78–79; follow-up care in, 89; and
    hormone therapy, 85, 87–88; nipple-
    areola complex in, 87–88; positioning of
    implant in, 79, 80, 82, 88; profile of
    implant in, 79, 86; recovery time in, 88;
    revision of, 82, 89; saline implant in, 79,
    85–86; selection of surgeon for, 85, 99;
    silicone implant in, 79, 85–86; size of
    implant in, 79, 86–87; at time of gender
    reassignment surgery, 76–77, 88–89
Building the Next Generation of Academic
    Physicians (BNGAP), 184
business and professional relationships:
    acceptance in, 129, 140, 176–177, 184–187;
    bias in, 153; and breast augmentation,
    88; communication in, 174; difficulties
    in, 54–55, 59, 81, 128–129; diversity and
    inclusion in, 185; and facial feminization
    surgery, 54–55, 59; and financial
    planning, 122; during first transition
    steps, 37, 43; gender inequality in, 153,
    177; and retirement, 137–138

California Dental Association, 55
cancer diagnosis: in friend, emotional
    impact of, 151–152; as trigger event,
    35, 36
Capote, Truman, 5

ABOUT THE AUTHOR

DR. ANNE L. KOCH received both her DMD and Certificate in Endodontics from the University of Pennsylvania. She is also the founder and past Director of the Postdoctoral Program in Endodontics and Endodontic Microsurgery at the Harvard School of Dental Medicine. Following her clinical and academic career, "Annie" formed her own successful technology and development company, Real World Endo, of which she was CEO and President. The author of more than one hundred and fifty articles in her specialty field, Dr. Koch has presented more than one thousand lectures worldwide. Dr. Koch is the holder of multiple patents and maintains a faculty position at PENN (Department of Endodontics) and serves as a Senior Fellow with Penn Medicine. She is also a member of the Board of Overseers for the University of Pennsylvania School of Dental Medicine. Additionally, she maintains an adjunct faculty position at the Harvard School of Dental Medicine.